The Watchdogs of Wall Street

Other Books by the author

BUY NOW, PAY LATER *1961*

THE THIEF IN THE WHITE COLLAR *(with Norman Jaspan) 1960*

THE ROYAL VULTURES *(with Sam Kolman) 1958*

Hillel Black

WILLIAM MORROW AND COMPANY

NEW YORK   1962

THE
WATCHDOGS
OF
WALL STREET

Library of Congress Catalog Card Number 62-16648

for Milt,

Jean Rae,

Eben,

Jonah and

Abigail

CONTENTS

The Watchdogs of Wall Street

1. 1929 AND NOW

A major object of this book will be achieved in what may seem like a paradoxical manner. The reader will encounter deceptions on a grand scale. He will meet among others a master stock salesman who during the uranium boom deceived not only the financial world but ultimately caused millions of dollars in losses to thousands of customers. He will be shown how the organized underworld invaded Wall Street and he will become acquainted with the inner machinations of the most brilliant corporate manipulator since Ivar Kreuger. He will meet, too, the son of a Czarist general who eventually controlled a financial empire that included three companies listed on the New York Stock Exchange and who could count among his accomplishments a phone call that was to cost the treasury of the late Dominican dictator, Rafael Trujillo, three-quarters of a million dollars. Finally, he will review the career of a young man who, by the time he was twenty-six, dominated nine corporations, left four banks in an uproar and directed a successful securities manipulation on the American Stock Exchange. These and other machinations of the past ten years probably cost the investing public at least one-half billion dollars.

The totality of these frauds may leave the reader with the impression that Wall Street has not renounced the wiles which it employed during the 1920's. Nothing could be further from the truth. For the ethics currently practiced by the vast majority of those whose business is Wall Street are exemplary. A brief history of the chicanery that occurred during the 1920's, and what resulted, will help show why Wall Street today may be considered a world with a viable conscience.

A number of authors have found understandable fascination in the speculative orgy and the crash of the stock market of little more than three decades ago. Interest was aroused by the spectacle of a market where the pigs overwhelmed the bulls and bears, the drama of fortunes lost overnight, the tragedy of the Depression. One aspect of these catastrophic events that proved particularly disturbing was the depredations practiced by most, though not all, of Wall Street on the American public. The magnitude of the deceits was revealed only after the machine lay inert and its inner workings were bared. The public was then treated through the hearing rooms of Congress to the rare view of financial cannibalism in its most unsavory form.

Several years after the debacle, Congress dissected some of the things that had taken place during the euphoric years. After noting that fully half of the $50 billion in new securities floated in the United States in the 1920's had become worthless, the House of Representatives declared in its report:

These cold figures spell tragedy in the lives of thousands of individuals who invested their life savings, accumulated after years of effort, in these worthless securities. The flotation of such a mass of essentially fraudulent securities was made possible because of the complete abandonment by many underwriters and dealers in securities of those standards of fair, honest and prudent dealing that should be basic to the encouragement of investment in any enterprise. Alluring promises of vast wealth were freely made with little or no attempt to bring to the investor's attention those facts essential to estimating the worth of any security. High-pressure salesmanship rather than careful counsel was the rule in this most dangerous of enterprises.

Typical of such operations was the flotation of three bond issues by the National City Company, the security affiliate of the National City Bank, for the Republic of Peru. The bonds, issued in 1927 and 1928, brought in $90 million. By 1931, they were in default. However, at no time was the public told that Peru possessed a dismal debt record, that it was an "adverse moral and political risk," and that its budget was perennially unbalanced, all of which information had been previously gathered and dutifully supplied to National City by its own officials.

These deceptions were equalled by the manipulations that occurred on the securities exchanges themselves. One of the more nefarious and certainly lucrative schemes was the famous pool operation. There the market price of a security was manipulated upwards by pool operators who, when the desired level was reached, dumped the securities at the higher price on the unsuspecting public. Organized support for the issue would then be withdrawn and the price would quietly drop. During 1929 alone, 107 stocks listed on the New York Stock Exchange were subject to one or more pools. They included such famous names in American business as American Telegraph and Telephone, American Tobacco, Gimbel Bros., Curtiss-Wright, Goodrich, Radio Corporation, Safeway Stores, to mention only a few.

Though not all pools were successful, many netted their originators and managers millions in profits. One of the more substantial manipulations involved The Sinclair Consolidated Oil Corporation. Starting on October 24, 1928, and ending on May 17, 1929, the pool managed to give the participants a profit of nearly $13 million, with only one member putting up any money for the purchase of the original stock. Among those partaking in this largesse were such notables as the Chase Securities Corporation, the securities affiliate of the Chase National Bank; Shermar Corporation, a private corporation owned by the family of Albert H. Wiggin, chairman of the governing board of the Chase National Bank; Harry F. Sinclair, chairman of the Executive Committee of The Sinclair Consolidated Oil Corporation; and the ineffable market operator, Arthur W. Cutten, a member of the Chicago Board of Trade.

What made these manipulations so shocking was the public stature of those who eagerly participated in them. Not only did some of the nation's most respected bankers join pools, but so did a large number of the major brokerage houses on Wall Street. Congress was to learn that between January 1, 1929, and August 31, 1933, some 175 member firms of the New York Stock Exchange participated in syndicates, pools or joint accounts. This did not include numerous member and non-member partners as well as individual members.

The public rarely if ever knew which stock issues were being manipulated. Much of the rise in prices could be attributed to brokers who were authorized by the pool to execute the appropriate buy and sell orders. The result was that the ordinary investor was sucked into the market through the false impression that others like him were favoring the particular security. This market activity was augmented by the dissemination of information favorable to the manipulated security.

Methods used to entice the public included the distribution of glittering market letters by brokerage houses, the employment of publicity agents, the dissemination of "tipster sheets" by supposedly reputable financial services and finally the subsidization of financial writers.

One of the most capable publicity agents at the time was David M. Lion, the publisher of *The Stock and Bond Reporter*. A major function of this paper was to publicize stocks that were involved in pools. Perhaps Lion's most successful venture was the hiring of William J. McMahon, a radio broadcaster who was billed as the president of the McMahon Institute of Financial Research. At the end of each broadcast which supposedly consisted of an objective discussion of the market, McMahon would boost the latest security that was being manipulated. For these services he received $250 a week. Lion's remuneration was a good deal larger. Between 1928 and 1930 he received a net profit of a half-million dollars. This was his compensation for publicity work he had done in connection with 250 manipulations.

Even more startling was the handiwork of John J. Levenson, a free-lance trader, who netted a profit of more than one million dollars from May, 1929, through March, 1930. Levenson's operations were aided by Raleigh T. Curtis, a financial columnist for the *New York Daily News* who wrote under the name of The Trader. Curtis' supposedly impartial reports on the stock market were spiced with helpful "tips" to his readers, lauding the stock issues in which

Levenson was interested. The columnist, in turn, received more than $19,000 from trading accounts in stocks he had dutifully touted.

Further evidence was presented by Fiorello La Guardia, then a Congressman, who exposed a publicity man by the name of Plummer. Plummer, according to the late New York Mayor, had distributed $286,279 for the publication of articles in the newspapers that boosted pool-inspired stocks.

This fraternal spirit of amorality found its lowest expression among the nation's most august financial leaders. One of the niceties of the time was the preferred lists of J. P. Morgan and Company, Wall Street's honored and famous banking house. The House of Morgan would set aside at the low original offering price securities they were underwriting. The recipients of these gifts were the nation's leading financial, industrial and political figures. Since these underwritings received considerable publicity, the market values quickly rose above the initial offering price. A few of those who received this largesse from just one Morgan offering, the common stock of Allegheny Corporation, included Charles Francis Adams, Secretary of the Navy; William Woodin, president of the American Car & Foundry Co. and later Secretary of the U. S. Treasury; Silas H. Strawn, president of the U. S. Chamber of Commerce and president of the American Bar Association; Joseph Nutt, treasurer of the Republican National Committee; Edmund Machold, speaker of the Assembly of New York State and chairman of that state's Republican Party; and John J. Raskob, chairman of the National Democratic Committee.

Raskob's name gained additional prominence as the result of a letter he wrote to George Whitney, a Morgan partner.

Whitney had reserved two thousand shares of Allegheny Common for Raskob at the original offering price of $20 a share. The letter follows:

Whitehall, Palm Beach

Dear George:

Many thanks for your trouble and for so kindly remembering me. My check for $40,000 is enclosed herewith in payment for the Allegheny stock, which kindly have issued when ready, in the name of John J. Raskob, Wilmington, Del. I appreciate deeply the courtesies shown me by you and your partners, *and sincerely hope the future holds opportunity for me to reciprocate.** The weather is fine and I am thoroughly enjoying golf and sunshine.

Best regards and good luck.

John

The day Raskob's letter was written, the price of Allegheny Common had already climbed to more than $33 a share. Within five months it was to reach as high as $57 a share, an increase of almost 200 per cent from the initial offering price.

The United States Senate Banking and Currency Committee, from whose hearings the above material was gathered, commented in its final report on the signficance of the preferred lists:

The granting of these preferential participations on the one hand and their acceptance on the other created a community of interest and similarity of viewpoint between donor and donee which augured well for their mutual welfare and ill for that of the public. Where officials of financial institutions which invest heavily in securities accept such favors, it is plain that the temptation exists to reciprocate directly by exercising their power to pur-

* Italics supplied.

chase securities from the bankers on behalf of their institutions without regard to the nature of the risk. By virtue of the influence gained by granting of favors to persons who hold multiple directorships in important corporations the bankers are enabled to exercise substantial control over the affairs and resources of those corporations. Public officials who consent to participate in "preferred lists" swiftly find themselves in a position where their usefulness is seriously impaired and they incur the danger of forfeiting the respect of the public.

The Senate Committee concluded its comments by declaring with notable restraint, "The 'preferred lists,' with all their grave implications, cast a shadow over the entire financial scene."

These manipulative and questionable practices were to reach their greatest intensity during the orgiastic year of 1929. Though the subsequent panic began on October 24 of that year, it wasn't until December 14, 1931, two years later, that the U. S. Senate passed a resolution calling for a major investigation of the securities market.

How the investigation actually came about is one of those ironies of history which, to this writer's knowledge, has so far never been reported.* Frederic C. Walcott, a Republican Senator from Connecticut, had received information that a group of Wall Street traders of the Democratic persuasion were purportedly planning a series of bear raids. Their intention, supposedly, was to lower prices further on an already depressed market, an event which, according to the intelligence received, would be used to help defeat President Hoover's bid for re-election in the fall of 1932. After a con-

---

* The source for this information is Ferdinand Pecora, who later served as counsel for the Senate Banking and Currency Committee, and as one of the original Securities and Exchange Commissioners. Judge Pecora was and is a Democrat.

ference with Walcott it was decided that the plans of these short-sellers could be exposed and thwarted through the medium of a public hearing. As a result of the passage of the Senate resolution, the Banking and Currency Committee began its investigation on April 11, 1932. Nothing was found to show that bear raids had been conducted by short-sellers in the week prior to April 11, the period during which an extensive campaign was supposed to have taken place. However, the Committee did uncover evidence dating back to the 1920's of such practices as pools, the subsidizing of newspaper men, the misuse of inside information by corporation officers, and the manipulation of the affairs of trading corporations and investment trusts. This information, though fairly extensive, was to prove only a preliminary exhumation. The more impressive finds were still to come.

Following the election of Franklin Delano Roosevelt in the fall of 1932, Senator Peter Norbeck, a Republican from South Dakota, and head of the Committee, called in Ferdinand Pecora as counsel. Pecora, a former Bull Moose Republican turned Democrat, had served as an assistant district attorney for New York County. A dark, handsome man with thick gray-black hair, Pecora was to add the scope and depth needed in the investigation. For the next year and a half, this Sicilian immigrant was to face the mightiest and most powerful men in Wall Street. How Pecora fared was later described by John T. Flynn, a financial journalist, who wrote: "I looked with astonishment at this man who, through the intricate mazes of banking, syndicates, market deals, chicanery of all sorts, and in a field new to him, never forgot a name, never made an error in a figure, and never lost his temper." Pecora, I might add, generally had the support of both Republicans and Democrats alike, especially that of Senator Duncan U. Fletcher, a Democrat from Florida, and the new chairman of the Committee.

To obtain some glimmer of what those days were like, I called on Pecora in his Manhattan office. Though nearing eighty, he was deeply involved in the private practice of law, going to court, still singularly alert, and, despite the years of harsh political battle in which he had subsequently engaged, judicious in judgment. His memory of those eventful days of 1933 and 1934 was vivid.

Judge Pecora told me that shortly after he had been called to Washington in January, 1933, to take over as counsel of the Senate Committee, he was asked by Senator Norbeck if he could really show how the people of South Dakota had been fleeced by the financiers. "I recalled," Judge Pecora added, "that I had read a recent item in the newspapers that the Insull bankruptcy records were in Chicago. I told the Senator the evidence could be supplied and sent investigators to Chicago to get the Insull records. The hearing was scheduled, but the records were delayed in arriving. I finally got them the night before. I kept reading and drinking coffee to stay awake. I studied till 5 AM. At 10 AM. we proceeded with the first witness."

As the result of Pecora's questioning and the evidence brought forth, the tissue construction of the vast Insull utility empire and the chicanery of the Street were thoroughly exposed. At the request of President Roosevelt and Justice Louis Brandeis, Pecora eventually wrote a book entitled *Wall Street Under Oath,* a vivid description of what had transpired on the Street during the lawless years.

"The testimony," he declared, "had brought to light a shocking corruption in our banking system, a widespread repudiation of old-fashioned standards of honesty and fair dealing in the creation and sale of securities, and a merciless exploitation of the vicious possibilities of intricate corporate chicanery."

But the testimony, he was able to note, had also helped bring reform. "The old regime of unlimited license," wrote Pecora in 1939, "may be said to have definitely come to an end."

The reform laws that grew out of the hearings insured that honesty and fair dealing would become the way of the Street. Further, these acts accomplished this in a manner that was totally in keeping with a free economy. In effect, they allowed Wall Street and the Federal Government to act as joint watchdogs so that the public could rightfully gain confidence in that area of business which may be fairly described as the heart of our economic well-being.

The two major reform laws which helped bring all this to pass and with which this book is concerned are the Securities Acts of 1933 and the Securities Exchange Act of 1934.* One of the reasons the deceptions and manipulations of the 1920's were so extensive was the absence of these Acts. Further, an understanding of how they work will help make clear the difference between the securities swindles of today and the machinations of the 1920's and early 1930's. First, let us examine the Securities Act of 1933, dry sounding in name but exciting in concept.

The "Truth in Securities" bill, as it has come to be known, was enacted four years after the crash. It is similar to a labeling act whereby the seller must tell the purchaser just what's in the product he is buying. In this case the product,

---

* Another reform law of utmost importance was the Glass-Steagall Banking Act passed by Congress in June, 1933. This act divorced commercial banks from their security affiliates and investment banks from their deposit business.

that is a company or corporation, is represented by stocks or bonds. In other words, the people who sell securities to the public must fully disclose the true facts concerning the operations of the company the securities represent.*

Thus, the company that raises money by selling newly issued stock to the public must make a full disclosure of how well the company is doing. This information must include a description of the company's assets, its debts and its prospects. Full disclosure of the facts must be made to the Securities and Exchange Commission, a Federal agency. These facts in turn must be disclosed to the public in a prospectus, a printed pamphlet that is generally a shorter version of the registration statement filed with the Commission.

The reasoning behind the "full disclosure" principle and the singular characteristics of stocks themselves were described in *The Work of the Securities and Exchange Commission,* a booklet published by the S.E.C.

"Securities," it was noted, "are by their very nature much different from most any other type of 'merchandise' for which there are established public markets. A person who wishes to purchase a new car or household appliance—or for that matter, a peck of potatoes or a bag of beans—can pretty well determine from personal inspection the quality of the product and the reasonableness of the price in relation to other competing products. But this is not so with respect to a bond or share of stock. An engraved certificate representing an interest in an abandoned mine or a defunct gadget manufacturer, for example, might look no less impressive

---

* Compulsory disclosure in the sale of securities originated in England when Parliament passed such a law in 1844, nearly ninety years before Congress enacted similar legislation.

than a 'blue chip' security with a history of years of un-broken dividend payments."

The S.E.C. pointed out that the only way the average investor can judge the true worth of securities is either through personal inspection of the company which issued the stock, often a virtual impossibility, or by relying upon oral and written reports describing the company and its prospects.

Though the S.E.C. demands a "full disclosure" of the facts on an issuing company's operations when it is filing a regis-tration statement, the Federal Commission *does not pass judgment on the value of the securities.* Judgment is left up to the investor. As the S.E.C. noted: "The Commission is powerless to pass upon the merits of securities; and assuming proper disclosure of the financial and other information essential to informed investment analysis, the Commission cannot bar the sale of securities which such analysis may show to be of little or no value."

This point is crucial. Under the Securities Act, a company may sell shares in its plan to offer a trip to the moon, even though the company has only a blueprint and is already one million dollars in debt. But it must be honest in its represen-tations to both the S.E.C. and the public. To put it another way, under the law a promoter can sell worthless stock in a bankrupt firm, but its true condition must be clearly labeled and described.

The Securities Exchange Act of 1934 not only extended the "full disclosure" doctrine of the 1933 Act, but outlawed manipulations on and off the stock exchanges. Thus, anyone participating in a pool or any other deceitful practice would be violating a Federal law. In addition the full disclosure principle was broadened to include trading by insiders—officers, directors and 10 per cent (beneficial) owners—who possessed stock listed on an exchange. This means the president of a company, for example, must file monthly reports with both the exchange and the Securities and Exchange Commission showing his holding in the company he is connected with. He must also report whether he has bought or sold those securities within the month's time and pay back to his company (the issuer of the securities) all profits made from transactions that occurred within a six-month period. These provisions were aimed at the misuse of "inside" information by the managers and beneficial owners of a company, an abuse prevalent in the 1920's.

The 1934 Act also called for complete disclosure by all companies with securities listed on an exchange. At this writing all companies with securities fully listed on the New York Stock Exchange as well as twelve other exchanges must file annual and other periodic reports disclosing the information which the investing public needs in evaluating the company's securities.

The Securities Exchange Act, as its title implies, also gives the Commission power to regulate the stock exchanges. The exchanges, under the law, must register with the Commission. To do so, exchanges must show that their rules will insure fair dealings to investors. The exchanges must also have the power to discipline members for conduct inconsistent with the rules of fair play. This includes the power to expel a member. While the exchanges can make their own rules, the Commission has the right to "alter or supplement" them. In practice, new rules or revisions are instituted after informal discussion between representatives of an exchange and the Commission. (At this writing there are thirteen national securities exchanges registered with the Securities and Exchange Commission.)

This system of self-regulation was extended to over-the-counter markets, through the creation of the National Association of Securities Dealers (N.A.S.D.), a self-policing organization which watches over the activities of dealers who buy, sell and trade securities off the exchanges. In addition, brokers and dealers must register with the S.E.C. The Commission, in turn, may deny or revoke a broker-dealer's registration in cases of fraud or other misconduct. On similar grounds it may also suspend or expel members of the N.A.S.D. or an exchange.

With the passage of these two Acts and others by Congress the Securities and Exchange Commission, a Federal agency, was given the power to regulate nearly all of Wall Street's activities.* This power is substantial. In the course of an investigation the Commission may take testimony under oath and subpoena books and records. Further, it may call upon the Federal courts to order an individual or firm to stop a particular fraudulent practice. Finally, it may call on the Justice Department to undertake criminal prosecution if evidence gathered by the Commission establishes that any individual or company has participated in a securities fraud, manipulation or other misconduct.

With this information in mind, let us return to the Street as we know it now and as it was in the 1920's. One basic difference is that Wall Street has had a policeman on the corner since 1934, protection which simply did not exist

---

* Other laws administered by the Securities and Exchange Commission include the Public Utility Holding Company Act of 1935, the Trust Indenture Act of 1939, the Investment Company Act of 1940 and the Investment Advisers Act of 1940. The S.E.C. also serves as advisers to the court under the Bankruptcy Act, Chapter X.

before then. Further, much of the chicanery that took place during the 1920's was legal. Today it is illegal. During the lawless years, for example, some citizens found the activities of the pool operator reprehensible, but there was nothing they could do about it. Today, the Federal Government would undoubtedly start criminal prosecution and the pool operator would probably find himself in jail.

Additional protection is given to the public through the change in attitude of Wall Street itself. As was noted earlier, the deceptions of the 1920's, though on a grand scale, were common. However, the men who practiced them were uncommon in power and public esteem. The succeeding improvement in ethical standards came about through the influx of a new breed of men as well as a change of heart in the old.

A graphic story that illustrates how many in Wall Street could learn new ways was the reformation of Joseph P. Kennedy, the father of the President. In June, 1933, the elder Kennedy joined in what was to be one of the last pools in Wall Street, the manipulation of the stock of Libby-Owens-Ford Glass Company. The pool was aided by the whimsical but fallacious belief on the part of the public that the company made glass bottles and thus would be increasing its business with the repeal of Prohibition. One year later, with the passage of the Securities Exchange Act, President Roosevelt appointed the elder Kennedy as one of the S.E.C.'s five commissioners. Roosevelt was not unaware of Kennedy's talents and it was, in fact, one of the reasons why he was offered the position. As it turned out F.D.R. had made a wise choice. For as the first chairman of the Commission, Joseph Kennedy ably and conscientiously applied his personal knowledge of the ways of the Street to help create the codes by which those ways would be permanently changed.

We now may bring up again our seemingly paradoxical proposition that the integrity of Wall Street can be described through an accounting of the modern securities swindlers and how they operate. For it should become apparent that these are not the men who belong to the Street, but those who raid it, with rare exceptions the outsiders, the pirates and buccaneers.

The reader will also discover how these modern securities swindlers were exposed. He will be taken behind the scenes of the S.E.C.'s New York Regional office and the Washington office's Special Investigations Unit, the Commission's front-line watchdogs. He will read about the unusual detective work and the problems the government investigators face as they hunt down the securities swindler. He will see, too, how these special sleuths solve what may be the most difficult crimes to unravel. These are crimes that divulge no fingerprints, no bullets, no corpses and rarely any witnesses. Unique in their complexity and world-wide ramifications, these crimes are committed by men of exceptional though twisted talents, men with great daring and resourcefulness who play a game where the stakes are counted in the millions.

2. THE KING OF PENNY STOCKS

ATTENTION INVESTORS!
Have you been wondering how you can best speculate with a small sum of money? Uranium! That's right! That's today's big opportunity. Just as automobile securities were the big opportunity for our fathers, and oil stock for our grandfathers. And what uranium stock currently offers you an unusual chance to cash in on such an opportunity? Well, according to Tellier & Company, a firm which has been in the investment business for over twenty years, there's one lowpriced uranium stock that today stands head and shoulders above the rest—in growth and profit possibilities. It's Consolidated Uranium Mines common stock, and it currently sells for around One Dollar a share . . .

The foregoing advertisement, preceded by a blast on a bugle, was typical of the messages repeatedly broadcast over a New York City radio station in the summer months of 1954. This ad like the others was paid for by Tellier & Company, a broker-dealer. The purpose of these messages was the widespread sale of inexpensive, highly speculative common stocks. Those who responded were usually the unsophisticated and gullible. As the result of these ads and other high-pressure sales campaigns, over one hundred thousand people acquired more than one hundred million shares offered by Tellier's firm. In the end they lost an estimated $25 million.

The man responsible for much of this debacle was a slightly balding former cosmetics salesman from Hartford, Connecticut, named Walter F. Tellier. As the underwriter or distributor of securities that usually sold for less than one dollar a share, he was the undisputed merchant king of "penny stocks." During the early and middle 1950's his firm, Tellier & Company, was one of the most active over-the-counter brokerage houses in the United States. Tellier himself was a prominent member of the National Association of Securities Dealers, a self-policing organization of the industry, the National Security Traders Association, and the Canadian Stock Exchange in Montreal. But behind this respectable facade Walter Tellier busily applied his talents to what has been alleged to have been one of the most odious series of securities swindles in the history of Wall Street.

Tellier's entrance into the securities business in 1925 was hardly auspicious. A seller of cosmetics, he became a bond and stock salesman, serving his apprenticeship in and around Hartford. In the aftermath of the 1929 crash, Tellier displayed his resourcefulness by retailing unlisted securities through the Morris Plan. Under this arrangement, he sold the stocks to his customers on a buy-now, pay-later basis. The customers, in turn, made their installment payments direct to the Morris Plan, which held the stock as collateral until the payments were completed. The plan, legal and commendable, was a forerunner of some of the time-buying schemes that were to sweep America following World War II.

Much later Tellier recalled those post-Depression days after the firm he was associated with foundered. "I had a couple of thousand dollars," he said. "In 1931 I started in business for myself in Hartford, Connecticut, and became pretty successful in selling issues for various New York houses. And about 1933 one of the Stock Exchange houses for whom I had distributed quite a few securities asked me to come to New York and open an office here and see if I couldn't get other brokers to distribute securities like I was doing and so [I] did open a branch office in New York in 1933. . . . My business in New York got so good, that I eventually closed the main office, and specialized in wholesaling securities to brokers, and established a very nice business."

It was about this time that Tellier had his first unpleasant experience with the law. His firm had become involved in the wholesale distribution of securities for Underwriters Group, Inc., which organized and sponsored a number of oil royalty-investment trusts. Tellier and about seventy-five others were indicted, the United States District Attorney charging "conspiracy and fraudulent pretenses circulated by mail and otherwise." Tellier, however, was not one of the principals and the indictment against him was dismissed.

Toward the end of World War II the nature of Tellier's business changed. Instead of selling high-priced oil properties and leases, he went into the business of merchandising speculative securities at under one dollar a share. In the sale of penny stocks he discovered his natural speciality. Probably no single stock broker and underwriter has been able to benefit so handsomely from the sale of shares at so inconsequential a price. Besides giving him a fortune, it allowed Tellier to possess all the assets of position and prestige that go to the most successful.

This soft-spoken man with the air of respectability managed to achieve such success because he had acquired the two essential traits of any supersalesman—showmanship and gall. A typical Tellier performance was his attendance at the annual conventions of the North American Securities Administrators, an association of officials whose jobs are to administer the Blue-Sky laws of the individual states and the Canadian Provinces. Arriving in a Cadillac, he would attend the meetings where he could listen to the Commissioners and others in the industry discuss the states' most urgent enforcement problems. His major contribution to these affairs was a lavish cocktail party which soon became the conventions' leading social event. What no one knew at the time was that while Tellier was wining and dining the state law enforcement officials, some of his salesmen were on the phone systematically deceiving the very people his guests had been assigned to protect.

Aware of the value of impressing others with his ability to make the right connections, he once hired the law partner of a White House aide whose job was to greet important visitors. A climber who shook all hands, Tellier, a lifelong Democrat, attended the 1952 Republican convention where he accompanied a politician into General Eisenhower's suite to offer greetings. Tellier later recalled the event:

"When we were going out the front door, the N.B.C. television was on the air, and my wife was with me, and we started to step out, and Ike started to step out at the same time, and he being the gentleman that he is, he stepped aside to let my wife go first, and so she was caught on a national hookup, with him just escorting her out the front door, for one second. That is as long as it lasted."

Tellier later implied that the S.E.C. started to hound him because of his wife's one-second television appearance with Eisenhower. Among other distinctions the king of penny stocks could claim the ultimate refinement of guilt by association.

Being in a way a man of his time, Tellier oozed respectability which he no doubt realized bred confidence. He became a reputable family man, acquired a handsome home in Englewood, New Jersey, and joined a Westchester Country Club, where, incidentally, he is reputed to have sold some of his soon-to-be-worthless stock to the clubhouse employees. Relying on the commercial axiom that the salesman can be more important in making a sale than the goods he is selling, Tellier made sure that his offices appeared prosperous and respectable, even though most of the merchandising was done over the phone or through the mails. On the apparent off chance that a few of his customers might call on him, he extensively remodeled his Jersey City office, having moved there from Manhattan's financial district in 1953 to avoid New York State taxes.

It was from the Jersey City office that his salesmen achieved their greatest success in selling the public on the virtues of Tellier offered stock. According to his own account he never discharged a salesman for misrepresentation and added that if a salesman refused to sell a security which he was offering, the salesman would be fired. "Either they sell Tellier merchandise or go," he once declared. As Paul Windels, Jr., the Government attorney who later prosecuted Tellier, noted, "He was not only the father of the modern boiler room, but his was the first wall-to-wall-carpeted operation." There was nothing seedy about Walter Tellier. Nothing, that is, except the securities he sold.

The plan that Tellier worked out whereby he could sell

to a mass market was accomplished in a methodical fashion. Like any retailer who is a pioneer merchandizer, the broker had to find the price the public wanted to pay for the securities he intended to sell. He also needed to seek out a sufficient number of eager and loyal customers who would hungrily come back for more. He solved the first problem of setting the "right" price by floating a number of oil, electronics and uranium issues at a cost to the buyer of a nickel to fifty cents a share. For some inexplicable reason the public preferred the fifteen-cents-a-share price tag.

While arriving at the right come-on price, Tellier busily built up a list of customers that eventually numbered 110,-000, of which 30,000 were considered active accounts. Reportedly the list is still in existence. Tellier sold it, so the story goes, to an investment-advisory service after the Government cracked down on his activities.

The methods he used to gather in the sheep were simple and direct. As previously noted, Tellier advertised extensively on the radio. He also placed ads in nearly all the New York newspapers: *The Times, The World Telegram, The Herald Tribune, The News,* and *The Mirror.* He even announced his offerings in the foreign-language press. The ads carried glowing accounts of his latest offerings plus a coupon whereby the prospective customer could send for information, listing, of course, his name and address. He managed to reach thousands of others through phone calls or via direct mail.

If you lived in Metropolitan New York during the middle 1950's and your hearing and eyesight were not impaired, you could not avoid knowing about Walter F. Tellier. For this publicity among the unemployed, the wage earners, the dreamers, the gullible, the ignorant and unsophisticated, the penny stockbroker spent as much as $10,000 a month, a small sum considering the results.

The really clever part of Tellier's operation was his apparent ability to abide by the law and still underwrite stocks or bonds that often were the riskiest speculations. The net effect of this scheme was to reverse the impact and purpose of the securities laws so that they protected him instead of his victims. The key to this plan consisted of making elaborate gestures of appearing to comply with the "full disclosure" principle of the Truth in Securities Act (1933) described in Chapter 1.

Crucial to Tellier's scheme was the small-issue exemption known as Regulation A. Designed to aid the small businessman, Regulation A exempts from full registration an issue of securities for which the total selling price for all shares is less than $300,000. The paperwork and lawyers' fees for securities sold under Regulation A are minimal. But, most important, the scrutiny sometimes given to Regulation A issues by the S.E.C. does not compare with the thorough investigations made on those issues which call for full registration.

Over the years Tellier filed more than one hundred issues with the S.E.C., most of them under the Regulation A exemption. As the underwriter selling these issues to the public, the broker was to average approximately $85,000 a month in commissions and money for his expenses. This meant that during a five-year period Tellier took in more than five million dollars as the initial seller of these penny stocks.

One of the ironies of the Tellier case is that his adept use of Regulation A made it almost impossible for the S.E.C. to bring him to justice. The prospectus, or offering circular, which the broker dutifully filed with the S.E.C. described the risks involved in the speculation Tellier was selling. However, the description would be written in technical language, often incomprehensible to the unsophisticated investors who made up the majority of Tellier's customers.

At the same time the underwriter sought to protect himself from any Government legal action that would result from the exaggerated claims made by his salesmen. He simply had printed on a number of the offering circulars this warning: "No dealer, salesman or other person has been authorized to give any information or to make any representation other than those contained in this Offering Circular, and if given or made, such information or representations must not be relied upon." Thus, a salesman could promise a customer that a fortune would accompany the purchase of Tellier-offered stock while the broker himself could claim that he personally was innocent of any wrongdoing.

Tellier's greatest success occurred during the uranium securities boom that followed the splitting of the atom. He not only was instrumental in helping the boom mushroom but was responsible for much of the ensuing fallout. Within a period of five years—from 1950 to 1955—Tellier & Company raised money for over forty uranium companies, virtually all of which turned out to be worthless. In the final debacle many investors could thank the broker for the loss of their life's savings. Among the perils born with the dawning of the Atomic Age, no one had envisioned the balding man from Hartford.

One such venture which proved most lucrative involved the underwriting of Consolidated Uranium Mines, a company incorporated in Nevada in 1950. The president of Consolidated was a man named Edward George Frawley, an old-time prospector who had searched much of the earth seeking his fortune in minerals and metals.

Tellier himself has offered his version of how he met Frawley, while testifying before a House subcommittee on Commerce and Finance in the fall of 1955. Declared the broker:

Tellier: Back in 1950 a man came from Salt Lake City, Mr. [Edward] George Frawley—and probably, when the fellow is dead, he will be given the credit as the man who really put America on its feet insofar as uranium production is concerned. But he came to New York City with a letter from a local Salt Lake banker to a banker in New York; that is generally the way it starts. The local banker in some neighborhood says to go to New York, "here is a letter to my banker."

In this case, Frawley went into the Commercial Trust Co., I believe, which is a big bank in New York, and got in touch with an officer in the bank, and the officer said, "Well, we can't do anything for you as a bank, but we do have a broker that handles a lot of securities for the bank, and I will get you an appointment with him."

So he made an appointment with a broker upstairs in the same building. The broker happened to be a stock-exchange firm.

Well, they looked the deal over, and they said, "It is out of our line." They are a regular stock-exchange firm and don't look at a deal unless it has net earnings of $300,000. You just can't get into a stock-exchange firm or a large underwriting firm unless you have those kind of figures to talk about.

They turned it over to one of the men in their organization who handled the mining stocks for that firm.

Well, of course, that man handled listed mining stocks. He had no outlet for unlisted new ventures. But he said, "I think I know a broker who could handle it for you."

Well, I happened to do my little stock-exchange business—the business that I do have—with that firm, and so they called me and said that there is a fellow here that has a mining deal, and we would like to have you look at it.

So he came over, and I looked at it.

QUESTION: Who was he?

TELLIER: He was Mr. [Edward] George Frawley, president of the Consolidated Uranium Mines.

QUESTION: That was your first deal?

TELLIER: That was the first deal.

I looked at it, and I listened to him, and I got all enthused about uranium. So I said, "I would like to know something about the business." Up to then I had been in the oil business and financing oil wells.

So he offered to take me back to Salt Lake City, and then we went to Grand Junction, and then to the property. I looked the property over to get an idea of what you can talk about. Then we looked around for an engineer to write a report, because I know that unless I could bring a geological or engineer's report into the S.E.C., I wouldn't have a chance to get it qualified.

So we went around and finally found a fellow that was working for Climax Molybdenum, and they formed a subsidiary called Climax Uranium, and I wanted to get a fellow with a little background to write the report so it would have some weight to it because I knew nothing about uranium.

He wrote the report, and we came back to New York, and I took him to an attorney and we set up a deal. We took it down to the S.E.C., and at that time it was brand-new, and we didn't have much problem getting it through because they didn't know too much about it, and the only thing they did as usual was this engineer said a few good things about it, and it went right out of prospectus. So we just said it was no good and had no prospects of finding any uranium, and it may never produce, and offered it strictly as a speculation, and so we got it cleared.

They critcized the engineer, but I searched all over and I couldn't find an engineer that had more than a couple of years experience in uranium.

QUESTION: How much experience did this fellow have?

TELLIER: He had about a year. He had just got out of school, and went into it. But he knew what he was doing. So anyhow, we financed that deal.

QUESTION: Was that for $300,000?

TELLIER: That was a $300,000 deal.

QUESTION: Did you sell the whole issue?

TELLIER: Yes.

The price the public paid was fifteen cents a share. Interestingly, Consolidated at that time could claim some value. In the first years of its operations the mining company had received nearly one-half million dollars from the Atomic Energy Commission for uranium and vanadium that was mined on leased property owned by the mining firm. However, over the succeeding years Consolidated securities were diluted to the point where despite any money the company made the stock itself was nearly worthless.

Between 1952 and 1954 Consolidated merged and absorbed five other uranium mining operations. These five corporations were in fact skeleton mining companies organized by Tellier's associates. The mining companies would buy up expiring uranium leases for a few hundred dollars. On the basis of these leases, Tellier would file a prospectus under Regulation A with the S.E.C. and then proceed to sell the penny stock to the public. Each sale would bring in about $300,000. After an appropriate time had passed, these mining companies, most of which produced little or no ore, would be taken over by Consolidated. Consolidated received the money raised by the underwritings of the five smaller uranium companies. At the same time the so-called assets or leases of these companies, which were generally worthless to begin with, were allowed to expire.

Tellier himself, it should be noted, did not actually own Consolidated Uranium. However, as the result of the mergers with the companies controlled by his associates, Tellier's people acquired thousands of shares of Consolidated Uranium, the mergers with the five companies being based on an exchange of stock. Tellier proceeded to trade the Consolidated stock through his brokerage firm, selling it to the public or other brokers at a handsome profit.

The broker managed to inflate the price of Consolidated stock by the age-old technique of puff and promise. Typical was this memo Tellier & Company sent to fellow dealers to interest them in pushing Consolidated. The memo was sent shortly before the mergers.

September 8, 1954

MEMO TO DEALERS ONLY
Re: CONSOLIDATED URANIUM MINES, INC.

This company owns 25,000 acres of Uranium leases in the Colorado Plateau area and will shortly announce the acquisition of 60,000 more acres via the merger of 5 companies into Consolidated (4 publicly owned and 1 privately). Also in this merger Consolidated will acquire machinery and equipment valued at over $200,000 and about $600,000 in cash.

Consolidated is now one of the largest producers of uranium ore and soon with the completion of a tungsten mill now building and another tungsten mill leased from Newmont Mining Co. it is believed they will also be one of the largest producers and refiners of tungsten.

Consolidated has produced and shipped about 4 million dollars worth of Uranium Ore and this has come from about 3 claims, just 60 acres, and production is still coming from these 3 claims. No man living can predict how much uranium will come from Consolidated's 85,000 acres and if any of the so-called uranium experts try to underrate this—

just tell him about the $4 million from 60 acres and you might mention that Floyd Odlum paid $9 million for about 10 claims (200 acres).

I personally believe Consolidated will sell through $5 per share—just give it time to develop—if you would like to make some money, buy Consolidated Uranium Mines, Inc., now at around $1.60 per share and start thinking of that $5 figure.

America is still a great country—whoever thought 41 years ago that $10,000 invested in what is today General Motors would be worth about $9,000,000. The Atomic Age stands today where the industrial age did when the present blue chips were mostly speculations.

We invite you to consider trading Con U—the most active over-the-counter uranium stock we know of. Send for details.
TELLIER & CO.

As the mergers headed toward consummation, Tellier's firm busily sent letters to customers advising them to buy up the remaining shares of the smaller uranium companies that were to be absorbed by Consolidated. The net result would be that the monies dumped into the smaller companies would end up in the coffers of Consolidated Uranium, thus raising the value of that firm's assets.

Between April and December, 1954, Tellier's printing and mailing machines whirred at full speed, preparing reports, bulletins and pamphlets that touted the mining company's stock. Tellier went so far as to write his customers: "If you have a friend or relative that you wish to give an everlasting Xmas gift to—give Consolidated because in a few years we still believe Consolidated will sell at $10 to $20 per share." And in another letter he declared, "Your children may enjoy it most—so put one or two thousand shares of Consolidated away for them."

Perhaps Tellier's wildest claim was addressed to the nation's registered broker-dealers. He wrote in a letter, "If you figure an acre of a uranium lease is worth $1,000.00 which is a reasonable average price, then Consolidated's 85,000 acres have a potential of 85 million, and there are only 14 million shares outstanding."

Less than a year later Frawley,* president of Consolidated, offered the following sworn testimony to the S.E.C.'s Edward Jaegerman in Salt Lake City, Utah.

JAEGERMAN: It was never intended that the Consolidated Uranium Mines, Inc. should ever own or operate or work 85,000 acres of leases?

FRAWLEY: No.

JAEGERMAN: That would be preposterous, wouldn't it?

FRAWLEY: Oh, yes; you wouldn't have enough money. You couldn't raise—

JAEGERMAN: And it costs a substantial amount of money per month just to do the necessary minimum amount of work to hold the leases?

FRAWLEY: Yes, it does.

JAEGERMAN: You might amplify that for the record, if you will?

FRAWLEY: Yes. The cost of holding these large areas, which we term prospecting areas, is very expensive, due to the fact that at least $100 per claim of 20 acres must be expended each year in order to hold such properties.

JAEGERMAN: The Consolidated Uranium Mines, Inc. never had the funds nor the source of funds to actively retain 85,000 acres?

FRAWLEY: Oh, no.

JAEGERMAN: And Mr. Tellier knew that, did he?

* Frawley has not been charged with any wrongdoing in connection with Consolidated Uranium and was not involved in any of the machinations that occurred.

FRAWLEY: He certainly should have.

JAEGERMAN: He was fully aware of the costs per year of maintaining an interest in a claim?

FRAWLEY: Yes, because he had been repeatedly advised.

JAEGERMAN: By you?

FRAWLEY: Yes.

At one point Tellier and some of his salesmen had inflated the price of Consolidated stock from fifteen cents to two dollars a share. Typical of the broker's profits was the sale of 250,000 shares for $1.87 per share. Tellier had originally bought the stock for one cent per share.

As the prices of the various uranium stocks went into orbit, a number of investors tried to turn their paper profits into cash by selling the stock back to Tellier & Company. But the investors almost invariably had difficulty taking their profits in dollars. The customers would be told by some of Tellier's salesmen to hold onto the shares. Of course, if the customer insisted on selling, the repurchased shares would then be sold to new customers sometimes at even higher prices.

On occasion certain Tellier salesmen would call customers who had bought shares at the initial low underwriting price. These customers would be given the opportunity to sell up to half their shares at double the price they paid for them. However, they would be dissuaded from taking their profits in cash. Instead, the purchasers were induced to invest the proceeds in Tellier's latest and newest offering. The traded shares taken from the old customers were then sold to new customers at even higher prices. For both the new and old customers it was just an endless merry-go-round and when the ride was finally over all they had to show for it was a drawer full of worthless stock certificates.

In the midst of these dubious activities, Tellier received an ironic encomium. In recognition of his success in selling uranium stocks, he was elected president of the Uranium Security Dealers Association.

Then, in November, 1955, the former cosmetics salesman was invited to appear before the Commerce and Finance sub-committee of the House of Representatives. The subcommittee at the time was attempting to learn whether investors in low-priced promotional securities needed more protection. The uranium boom, Tellier testified, had been deflated in recent months because of "The publicity from the pinks all over the country hollering 'fraud' from the rooftops, and 'phoney' this, that, and the other thing. If you ever wanted to try to ruin America's production of uranium, they almost did."

"Did you say 'pinks'?" the chairman of the subcommittee asked, his voice incredulous.

"Surely," replied Tellier. "All of those people are talking about fraud, and phoney. They don't know what they are talking about. They must be a little bit left or pink or something."

It was undoubtedly Walter F. Tellier's baldest hour. Though he did not know it at the time, it was also one of his last as the merchant king of penny stocks.

The stockbroker's activities were not completely unknown at the Securities and Exchange Commission. Complaints were growing, congressmen were pressing questions, caustic remarks could be heard on Wall Street and read in the financial pages. Harold C. Patterson, then director of the Division of Trading and Exchanges in Washington, sensed that the Commission was facing a crisis. He assigned Edward C. Jaegerman and John Timothy Callahan, the heads of the crack Special Investigations Unit, to look into Tellier's affairs.

In picking Jaegerman and Callahan the Commission was sending out the best it had. Both Yale graduates, they each had over twenty-five years experience detecting securities frauds. But most important, they possessed the highly developed instincts of the hunter who had the uncanny ability of seeking out seemingly invisible prey.

Though an ideal team and the S.E.C.'s top investigators, no two men are more dissimilar in appearance. Jaegerman, wiry, impetuous, his suits rumpled, is constantly in motion, even when he is supposed to be sitting still. On the other hand, Callahan, an immaculate dresser and former All-American football player, is invariably at ease no matter how great the pressure. Where Jaegerman uncovers fraud in the most complex financial statements, Callahan specializes in gently drawing damaging testimony from recalcitrant witnesses. The scourge of shady operators, they are known in the United States and Canada as "The Rover Boys."

Jaegerman and Callahan began their investigation by calling on Tellier at his office, then located in New York. Later Callahan recalled the interview at one of Tellier's subsequent trials. The interview revealed in detail not only Tellier's day-to-day operation, but it gave the investigators the lead that, ironically, was to prove the stockbroker's undoing.

Tellier, according to Callahan, told them that though his firm was a partnership, he was in absolute control and "that he had the last word in the selection of salesmen and supervised them and knew what they represented and said when they sold securities offered by his firm over the telephone." At that time Tellier had about twenty salesmen who worked from 10 A.M. to 8 or 9 P.M. Most of the firm's customers came from New York, New Jersey, and Pennsylvania. The stock-broker also told Callahan that he sold securities throughout the world and that he himself was about to make some seventy solicitations among potential customers who lived west of the Mississippi River. Most of his business, Tellier said, was done by telephone and by mail.

Then Callahan posed a seemingly innocuous but crucial question. "I asked him at this point," the investigator recalled, "to give me the names of the securities in which they had never paid a dividend, and he said the only one that paid a dividend was Alaska Telephone Corporation."

As the two investigators were about to leave, Callahan testified the following exchange took place:

"At the conclusion of the interview Mr. Tellier said, 'Now, I will co-operate with you if you will co-operate with me. I want you to give me the name of the person who is responsible for your coming here today, and if you don't tell me and I find out who it is, I will go out and I will break you.'

"I then told [him] we were there on the authority of the Commission. And Mr. Jaegerman and I left."

Callahan and Jaegerman had been with the S.E.C. for too many years to be concerned with Tellier's threat. What did intrigue them, however, was the stockbroker's admission that only one company he had underwritten had paid a dividend. The logical procedure would have been to start the investigation by checking any one of the *non*-dividend-paying companies, since the absence of dividends may be symptomatic of financial difficulty. Instead, instinct and perversity decided the two men to look into the one firm Tellier himself had said paid dividends, the Alaska Telephone Corporation.

Like many of the companies with which Tellier became

involved, Alaska Telephone Corporation started as a worthy and legitimate endeavor, to bring telephone service and electrical power to what was then the Territory of Alaska. The company, formed in 1948 by a small group of Western promoters, proceeded to purchase several telephone exchanges with about 700 subscribers. It wasn't long before they needed additional financing. Attempts to raise the money in Seattle, Washington, and Alaska, and to borrow it from the Federal Government met without success. So in April, 1951, Major William Maxey, then president of the corporation, came to New York. The office he and his associates finally arrived at was that of Walter Tellier.

It was part of Tellier's genius to recognize the sales potential of those industries and companies which would excite the imagination and whet the unsophisticated investor's financial appetite. A private utility in Alaska, the last frontier, possessed considerable promise. Understandably, Tellier agreed to underwrite the pioneering telephone company. To make the issue appear as attractive as possible, the broker decided to raise money by selling bonds instead of stocks. The twenty-year debentures would pay interest at one-half per cent each month. The bonds would sell for $100, $500, and $1,000, and could be converted into stock. Thus, for twenty years the purchasers would receive 6 per cent a year on their money, a reasonable return, and the stock conversion, if the company succeeded, would make them rich.

Tellier had one other suggestion. The name of the company originally was Alaska Telephone & Engineering Corporation. The stockbroker thought a better name would be Alaska Telephone & Telegraph Corporation, the A.T. & T. of Alaska. There was one drawback, however. The company did not own any telegraph facilities. On the advice of his attorneys, Tellier was persuaded that under the circumstances identification with the name of the world's largest phone company would never do. The fledgling utility would have to be called Alaska Telephone Corporation.

The offering circular for the first bond series, known as Series A, was filed at the regional office of the S.E.C. in Seattle as required by Regulation A. Then in September, 1951, Tellier & Co. began pumping the $299,500 issue into the market. Printed flyers and the pitch made by his salesmen emphasized that Alaska Telephone bonds were an absolutely secure investment, with a high rate of return, payable monthly. They went as far as to guarantee the interest and to claim that the debentures were gilt-edged, comparable to the securities of A.T. & T., Government Bonds and savings accounts. Within three months Tellier's men had sold the entire issue to over six hundred customers. As the result of the sale Tellier & Co. received $85,000 in underwriting fees. Meanwhile, Alaska Telephone, which was to sustain over $45,000 in operating losses in 1951, had just acquired an additional annual debt of $17,970, money which the phone company would have to pay each year to its new bondholders in the form of interest.

While the Series A bonds were being readied for merchandising, the management of Alaska Telephone passed into new hands. Elton P. Jones, the company's counsel, was named president. Jones had had a distinguished career. He had served three and a half years as an officer in the United States Navy, had been appointed a municipal judge, pro tem, of Seattle, and had been named to the International Pacific Salmon Fisheries Commission by the President of the United States. He also served as a public member of the Waterfront Securities Appeal Board for the Pacific Northwest, having been appointed by the Coast Guard Commandant. Jones shared the top management with a man named Albert Joseph Proctor, a neighbor, a respected citizen, a successful salesman and secretary of Alaska Telephone. Though neither man was to gain personally from the fast shuffle that was taking place, both played key roles in the developing conspiracy.

In the months following the sale of the Series A bonds, Alaska Telephone found itself going deeper into debt. To keep operating, the firm had used monies which had been witheld for income-tax purposes from the employees' pay as well as excise taxes which had been collected from subscribers to the telephone service. The private utility had also failed to turn over long-distance toll charges to Alaska Communications System, an Army installation which the phone company was permitted to use. Finally, starting in June 1952, Alaska Telephone Corporation was in continuous default in its indenture agreement with Colonial Trust Company, a New York bank which did the paper work and sent the interest checks to the bondholders. This agreement provided that Alaska Telephone would maintain on deposit with the bank an amount of cash sufficient to cover monthly interest payments to the bondholders for a six month period. The indenture further provided that in the event of a default in the prepayment requirement lasting sixty days, the bank, if it wished, could declare the face amount of the bonds due.

It was apparent that once more Alaska Telephone was in immediate need of funds. Again attempts were made to raise money in Seattle and Alaska, and again they failed. This time it was Proctor who came to see Tellier. Proctor insisted that Alaska Telephone had been steadily reducing its losses and that the last quarter of 1952 would show a profit. A former S.E.C. attorney hired by Tellier recommended that common stock be sold, thus saving the monthly interest payments. However, the lawyer was overruled by Tellier who insisted on the more salable bonds.

In April, 1953, about one and one-half years after the sale of Series A, Tellier began offering Series B bonds. When redeemed in ten years, Alaska Telephone would have to pay $150,000, the face amount of the debentures. Tellier, however, had sold them at 30 per cent discount, or a $100 bond for $70. Out of the $150,000 face amount of the Series B bonds, Alaska Telephone actually received only $60,000, most of the remaining sum being absorbed in a $45,000 discount and $25,000 in commissions and fees to Tellier & Co. As a result of the Series B sale, Alaska Telephone had increased the interest it had to pay each year to the bondholders to $29,970. Furthermore, Alaska Telephone had lost $98,000 in 1952, the year the phone company was supposed to "break even."

Conditions, of course, grew only more desperate and more financing was called for. The stockbroker's lawyer, who was to become a government witness, attempted to dissuade Tellier from further offerings. The attorney later testified in court:

THE WITNESS: I called Mr. Tellier and I said, Walter—in substance, you can't go ahead with any public offering in this case. It would involve you in great trouble. . . .

I said it seems to me now, looking back over the Series B issue, that what Alaska has been doing—Alaska Telephone—is selling bonds to stay alive, to keep going, as a substitute for earning money.

At the time of Series B issue, I told him—they told us they had broken even. It is now apparent from the figures attached here they did not break even. And they lost a lot more money in 1952.

I do not believe that either of these people is competent; that

Jones or Proctor is competent to run this company. I do not think it is reasonable to anticipate they will make any money.

On that basis, if you sell bonds, you are merely selling additional bonds instead of having the company make money. And this selling of bonds to pay back interest by the sale of new bonds will involve you in a Ponzi scheme.

THE COURT: P-O-N-Z-I?

THE WITNESS: Yes. I urge you not to sell any securities to the public at all. . . .

The lawyer informed Tellier he could no longer represent him. Tellier's answer was to bring out a $270,000 bond issue known as Series C. It was then April, 1954, and the broker's high-pressure salesmen had begun "boiling" the bonds over the phone. Sales, however, were not going at the same speed as previous issues.

On April 26, Proctor wrote Tellier: "Keep plugging, as we are certainly at a critical point in holding on to the properties."

Eight days later Tellier replied: "Every time you see any newspaper clippings of any kind, or any kind of publicity about any of the towns in Alaska where we have telephones, wish you would please send it to me. If it looks like something is going to create more telephone business we can get it offset and mailed to the bondholders. Sales, as you know, are slow and we need something to wake up the people."

Two days later Proctor wrote Tellier: "Please build a fire under your sales organization. As previously explained, we must make some cash settlements in the immediate future."

A number of Tellier's salesmen needed no urging as they telephoned the unsuspecting: a waiter, a school teacher, a printer, a postal worker. "You must act fast," the pitch went.

"It pays a good dividend. Comparable to A.T. & T. and Con. Ed. Gilt-edged. Interest is coming out of earnings. You can buy a bond a month on our bond-a-month plan." The purchasers, people of little or no financial experience and small means, were switched out of Government Bonds, savings accounts, postal savings, and in some instances their life's savings.

By midsummer, 1954, the Series C bonds had been sold out. Out of the proceeds Tellier received $41,500 as fees, expenses and repayment of his advances. Following the sale, Alaska Telephone's yearly bond-interest debt had risen to over $43,000. Three months later the phone company was in continuous default in its interest prepayments under the indentures for all three bond series. By the end of October, Proctor, who had replaced Jones as president, again traveled from Seattle to New York to seek still more financing. The proceeds from Series C had already been exhausted. While Jones, now Secretary-Treasurer, prepared a new offering circular, Tellier and his salesmen readied themselves to sell the final bond issue, Series D. It was to be a merchandising campaign of unbounded cynicism.

The selling began in December, 1954. Albert Schwartz, a postal employee at the Church Street Station in New York, later testified how he was induced to buy $500 worth of Series D Bonds:

SCHWARTZ: And then he [the salesman] asked me if I have any children. I said yes, I have two children. And then he suggested to take some bonds in their names. He says it was a good idea so in case . . .

QUESTION: Did he say why?

SCHWARTZ: Yes. He told me it will be like a nest egg for them and in future years you can have a college—if they went to college—education or use the money for other purposes. It will be a very good idea for them because it was a high interest paying.

And, well, I believed in them because I had confidence. I was getting my dividends from the Series C and everything was, you know, running smoothly.

And he says, well, how much could you afford?

I told him I didn't have much money. I had some Government Bonds, and he suggested that I cash them in because they were paying only three per cent, the bank, where I can get eight and a half per cent on the telephone bonds.

So I proceeded—I cashed in some of my bonds, and I used some of my children's money from their accounts in order to purchase Series D bonds.

Another customer was Charles Anello, a public school teacher in Upper Montclair, New Jersey. Mr. Anello had three children at the time. Charles Anello, spared none of the salesmen's usual exhortations, had the questionable privilege of speaking to Tellier himself. Shortly before Christmas, the schoolteacher testified, Tellier called him at his home. "It would be nice," Charles Anello quoted the broker as saying, "to have a bond hanging on the tree for the children—the Christmas tree. . . ."

The schoolteacher, who had bought $1,200 worth of Alaska Telephone bonds, was then asked by government counsel if he had ever taken business courses on the art of analyzing corporate balance sheets. Charles Anello replied regretfully, "I wish I had, sir."

With the sale of Series D, the New Jersey schoolteacher along with eighteen hundred other unsuspecting customers had bought a total of $900,000 worth of Alaska Telephone bonds, all of which eventually turned out to be worthless. As the underwriter, Tellier received $150,000 in fees and expenses. The broker himself had attempted, in the final moments, to perpetuate the illusion of solvency by advancing his own money to Colonial Trust to pay the interest charges which had risen to over $52,000 a year. In September, 1955, exactly four years since Tellier had first offered the bonds to the public, Colonial notified the bondholders that Alaska Telephone was in default and no further interest payments would be made. By November the telephone company had been placed in bankruptcy. On December 27, two days after Christmas, Tellier offered a bondholder $1.50 for a $100 Alaska Telephone bond. The bubble had burst.

Only a few days after Tellier appeared before the Congressional subcommittee, the S.E.C.'s Eddy Jaegerman arrived in the Brooklyn office of United States Attorney Leonard P. Moore. The Commission had previously consulted with the Justice Department in Washington, and was told that Moore and his staff had a reputation for handling difficult cases. Because many of Alaska Telephone's bond customers lived in Brooklyn and Long Island, the case fell within Moore's jurisdiction.

While Jaegerman settled himself in the U. S. Attorney's office, Moore called one of his assistants, Paul Windels, Jr. As Windels stepped into Moore's office he noticed an intense, alert man wedged in the corner of the sofa, his lap littered with documents. Then Eddy Jaegerman began to speak and Moore and Windels listened, fascinated. For the two men quickly realized the impact of the story that was unfolding. As one of the country's largest over-the-counter brokers, Walter F. Tellier was not only well-known on the Street but by brokers throughout the nation.

As soon as Jaegerman finished his discourse, Windels was assigned by Moore to work on the Federal grand jury presentment. It was the young attorney's first securities case. On

December 1, 1955, the grand jury returned criminal indictments against Tellier, Proctor, Jones, and what was left of Alaska Telephone Corporation. The broker and the respectable businessmen were charged with a total of thirty-six counts involving violations of the Securities Act and mail fraud.

Following the indictments, Windels joined Eddy Jaegerman and Harry Casagrande, an expert accountant from the New York State Attorney General's office, in a trip to Seattle to gather more information on Alaska Telephone. While there, Jaegerman suggested that they take a side trip and look into Consolidated Uranium. Later Windels, who had been an aerial observer in World War II, recalled their flying visit to the Colorado Plateau:

"I had the impression from reading all the literature Tellier had put out on Consolidated Uranium that this was a major mining operation. But from the air the mines appeared like gopher holes. When we landed and toured the place with Frawley I saw that most of the uranium ore was being mined by hand, loaded in big buckets and brought to the surface. There was no continuity in the runs of ore which lay in separate deposits like raisins in bread. Frawley told us he spent a good deal of his time fighting off poachers who would sneak onto the property with dump trucks and attempt to steal a little of the ore. This had been touted as a multimillion dollar operation. As we again circled the mining site in the airplane, the fraud was literally spread before our eyes."

Windels and Jaegerman had seen enough to realize that Consolidated Uranium had the makings of a much bigger case than Alaska Telephone. As the result of information presented by Moore, Windels and Jaegerman, a second Federal grand jury returned a criminal indictment against Tellier and six associates involving the sale of securities in seven mining ventures. Among them was Consolidated Uranium,* which has since gone out of business.

Meanwhile, the Supreme Court of New York, as the result of action taken by the State Attorney General, barred Tellier from selling securities in New York for five years. Two Federal trials followed, the first ending in a hung jury. But at the second trial Tellier, Proctor and Jones were convicted of violating the fraud section of the Securities Act (1933) and mail fraud. In April, 1957, Tellier was sentenced to four and one half years in prison and fined $18,000. Proctor and Jones received suspended sentences. The Federal prosecuting attorney was Paul Windels, Jr.

A footnote to the Tellier saga occurred shortly after sentencing and before United States District Judge Mortimer W. Byers set bail. Between the end of the second trial and the day he was sentenced, Tellier had made a business trip to Denver. Windels, in arguing against granting bail, told the court:

"If your Honor pleases, I believe that the facts set forth here demonstrate that Mr. Tellier has evinced a complete and thorough disrespect for the processes of this court and any obligation to which he is put.

"The fact that he went out to Denver purportedly in connection with a commercial transaction may have been told to Mr. Burke [Tellier's attorney], but I daresay he didn't tell Mr. Burke before he went what he was about, that he had threatened a witness who was before a grand jury in this district with bodily harm and that he finally wound up mak-

* At this writing Tellier is still awaiting trial on the uranium mining indictment.

ing a deposit of over a quarter of a million dollars in securities in a clear bribe of that witness. That, I believe, is sufficient basis to remand this defendant to the custody of the Marshal.

"Your Honor," Windels continued, "we have seen a number of defendants come and go in this courtroom—your Honor many more than I—but I can't see why simply because this defendant happens to find himself connected with a commercial fraud rather than a crime of violence that he should be given any particular consideration, and I think that the lack of any moral standards of this man was shown time and again during the trial.

"Your Honor, it was demonstrated that he lived with a business that was corrupt from beginning to end. This was not a crime that only took a few minutes to commit, this was a crime that went on, day after day, week after week, year after year.

"Mr. Tellier, as a part of his daily life, lived that crime."

Judge Byers, in granting $50,000 bail, declared, "You see, Mr. Windels, I wouldn't necessarily disagree with you as to the moral make-up of the defendant Tellier. Bail is exacted on the theory that a man will not evade the jurisdiction of the Court; he will appear on judgment day."

For a year Walter F. Tellier remained a free man while his attorney appealed the stockbroker's conviction. The United States Court of Appeal's upheld the jury's decision and in 1958 the Supreme Court declined to review the case. With no other legal recourse remaining open to him, the stockbroker boarded the train that took him to a Federal penitentiary in Atlanta.

Because Tellier had unwittingly crossed the path of an Assistant United States Attorney, some of the shrewdest

stock swindlers who ever ventured on the Street were to find
their days of financial legerdemain numbered. As a result
of the work he had done in preparing the Tellier indictments, Paul Windels, Jr., at the age of thirty-four, was named
head of the New York Regional Office of the Securities and
Exchange Commission. Like a physician's stethoscope the
New York office is the ear on the heart of the busiest and
most important securities market in the world. For the S.E.C.,
the selection of Windels was the Government's answer to the
mounting complaints emanating from the Street. For the
nation's most brazen and successful securities manipulators,
the young lawyer's appointment was to herald the end of an
era.

3. THE UNDERWORLD INVADES WALL STREET

It was late in the afternoon when Paul Windels, Jr., and Tim Callahan climbed to the loft of an old office building on lower Manhattan. As Callahan flung open the door and stepped inside, Windels quickly followed him into the room. A glance showed the floor of the loft littered with cigar butts, empty whiskey bottles and racing forms. Chairs consisting of upended boxes surrounded a table made of long planks and wooden horses. Flattened cardboard, nailed to the windows, barred the sun and air so that the room seemed to heave with the fetid smell of perspiration and drifting cigar smoke. The only lighting came from the garish reflection of bare bulbs that hung from the ceiling.

Seated shoulder to shoulder and around the table were a score of salesmen, many stripped to the waist, others in undershirts. Each man faced a phone and a soundproof cubicle the size of an egg crate. The soundproof cubicle blocked out the voices of the men nearby so that each salesman could give the illusion that he was calling from his own well-upholstered office. Above the modulated hubbub, the visitors noticed an older man lecturing a group of college-age youngsters.

As the two officials displayed their credentials, the room suddenly became silent. Then Callahan began the questioning, "Who are your coxeys, loaders, dynamiters?" Shrugs, followed by sworn denials. The questioning persisted. And then they talked. Haltingly at first. But they talked.

For Windels the raid was disturbing and startling. It was the first time he had actually seen a boiler room, the place where high-pressure salesmen sell nearly worthless securities over long-distance telephones. The raid proved equally disturbing for the boiler-room operators. A salesman who was there later recalled the event:

"We were working Great Sweet Grass at the time. It was a real big bust out. The stock was coming down from Canada and they were running a good strong market. There were about twenty of us on the phones in this place. Most were experienced loaders, good producers.

"We had been hearing about Windels from some of the Tellier boys who were called before the grand jury. Most of us old-timers knew of Tim Callahan. He is very big around and wears an Italian homburg. When the papers said Windels was going to be the S.E.C. chief here, we knew there would be trouble. Some of the boys slid out to see how things would go. But the smart boys said Tellier would beat his raps and everything would be fixed up. We had been really scoring and we thought there would be some time. Then the first damned day there was a bang on the door. Then it bounced open and in came Tim Callahan. He looked as big as a locomotive. And Windels was right with him. Absolutely, we were stupefied. Our office manager was the quickest man I ever knew with something to say. But he just stood there open-mouthed."

For Windels the day of the raid, August 6, 1956, became memorable for several reasons. Earlier in the day he had taken the oath as the new Regional Administrator of the New York office of the Securities and Exchange Commission.* After the usual exchange of pleasantries offered by the visiting Washington officials and representatives of the Street, Windels turned to Tim Callahan and whispered, "Let's go." Unknown to the dignitaries who had come for the ceremony, the two men had arranged to make the raid just described. It was Windels' first official act.

The initiative displayed by the new Administrator was not unexpected. As a former Assistant U. S. Attorney, Windels had shown himself to be unusually industrious. For the past few years he had been busy prosecuting a convicted abortionist charged with income-tax evasion, a truck driver who specialized in hijacking fountain pens, and an armed bank robber whose $190,000 theft set some sort of national criminal record as the largest one-man haul. He was also involved in limiting the freedom of underworld enforcers, dope peddlers and kidnapers. By the time he was thirty-four, the attorney had handled thirteen major trials and obtained convictions in almost every case. The Tellier affair had been his only experience involving securities frauds.

For the more artful stock swindlers such a record, though impressive, did not seem particularly unnerving. It is one thing to prosecute a bank robbery. It is another to unravel dummy accounts, corporate chicanery and a securities manip-

* Windels has returned to the private practice of law, having resigned from the S.E.C. in February, 1961.

ulation six times removed from the actual manipulator. Windels, however, was to produce a few surprises.

The son of a New York City Corporation Counsel and the late Mayor LaGuardia's campaign manager, Paul Windels, Jr. attended Princeton. His college days were interrupted by World War II. Joining the Army as a private, he saw action in Europe as an aerial observer for the Field Artillery and emerged a captain.

After graduating from Princeton, he went to Harvard Law School, then joined the Wall Street law firm of Wickes, Riddell, Bloomer, Jacobi & McGuire. His background and appearance, which include a penchant for vests, suspenders and horn-rimmed glasses, seemed to make him eminently suited for such sedate surroundings. As a lowly associate the young attorney was expected to spend most of his working hours in the firm's law library, digging up footnotes for other men's briefs.

On one occasion he had been chosen to do the preliminary work on a complicated reorganization case. Without advising the partners first, he took matters into his own hands and proceeded to incorporate a new firm. As one of the law firm's older attorney's noted, "This training process has different effects on the young men. Some of them turn out to be hypercautious. Others are apt to strain at the leash a bit. Paul Windels was the latter type."

Boredom and a desire to do something challenging ended Windels' career with the Wall Street law firm. After campaigning for President Eisenhower in 1952, he was named an Assistant under U. S. Attorney Leonard Moore, the new Republican appointed prosecutor for the Eastern District of New York. Though Moore was not unaware of political debts, the staff he himself handpicked were generally young men of outstanding capabilities and promise. As the head of the S.E.C.'s most important office outside of Washington, Windels would be forced sooner than he realized to show whether Moore's earlier judgment had been prescient.

The new Administrator's boiler-room raid with Tim Callahan was the first proof of what was to become a series of disturbing revelations. While preparing the Tellier case, Windels had received a number of tips of massive stock swindles emanating from Wall Street itself. Actually these occasional reports understated what was really taking place.

Later investigations were to show the American public had been victimized on an unbelievable scale. In 1956 alone, unscrupulous boiler-room salesmen swindled tens of thousands of people out of an estimated 150 million dollars. Their victims, as the result of high pressure selling by a practiced army of con men, had bought over 350 million dollars worth of nearly valueless stock from 1950 through 1956, when the swindles reached their height.

Further, some of the boiler rooms were located within one hundred yards of the New York Stock Exchange. One was uncovered only a few floors above the S.E.C.'s former New York Regional office. But perhaps most disturbing of all was the undeniable fact that the boiler rooms had opened the door to an invasion of Wall Street by the organized underworld. Though this infiltration was several years in coming, Windels, at the time he took office, found himself faced with a major law enforcement problem.

The campaign began in earnest the morning after the swearing-in ceremony. Bill Moran, a veteran S.E.C. enforcement lawyer and Assistant Regional Director, Jack Devaney, Moran's right hand man, and Jim Murray, chief of investigations, held their first staff meeting with their new boss. Windels discussed his visit of the previous day and made an immediate request for a list of all known or suspected boiler rooms operating within his jurisdiction. Twenty-four hours later the list was placed on his desk.

The list contained the names of more than thirty suspect brokerage houses, almost all of them located in the Wall Street area itself. While the primary targets were being selected, the entire office was reorganized into task forces consisting of investigators, accountants and attorneys. Each team would report directly to Moran who had drawn a battle plan on a blackboard in his office. The plan was simple. Seven to eight teams would be sent out each day on simultaneous raids. Since S.E.C. investigators are empowered under the securities laws to make unannounced periodic investigations of all registered broker-dealers and their books, the teams would be within their legal rights to inspect the questionable houses without search warrants. If they should run into trouble they would call Moran, who in turn authorized subpoenas based upon formal orders issued by the Commission in Washington. The boiler-room operators were then forced to turn over their books and other information necessary to the investigation.

On August 8, forty-eight hours after Windels had been sworn into office, the raiders struck. While a skeleton crew manned the office, the S.E.C. investigators, all unarmed, many in their fifties, formed their assigned squads and spread throughout the world's most famous financial district. Within minutes they began phoning their first reports to Bill Moran and his aides. By the end of the week an extraordinary tableau emerged. As related by Windels:

"We were to find some five hundred high-pressure boiler-room salesmen working in the different houses. They had come to New York from all over the United States and Canada. The Ivy League of penal institutions was fully represented with graduates of Alcatraz, Leavenworth, McNeil Island, Toronto Regional Jail and Sing Sing. On our first raid we found one salesman who was a two-time killer from Chicago. Seated right next to him was another who had served ten years on a narcotics charge. They were experts in the art of swindling, having been trained in the classic 'bait and switch' school, then graduating into the carnival game, and the home and farm repair rackets. I suppose you could say this was the greatest concentration of unique professional talent since the Manhattan Project."

These con men could be divided into three groups. The lowest strata were the coxeys or apprentice swindlers. A number of them turned out to be pre-med and law students working their way through college. "All of them," Windels noted, "were smart kids trying to break into the fast-buck business."

It was the coxeys who first approached the prospective victims, preparing them for the fleecing that was to come later. The coxeys worked off customer lists that were given to them by the boiler room's sales manager. The lists were frequently purchased from commercial houses that collected names for legitimate businesses seeking new customers. The boiler-room operators managed to obtain lists of Army sergeants, widows who had inherited sizable estates, doctors, dentists, teachers, and those already afflicted with the speculative fever. There were two classes of victims—the well-to-do who invested their excess cash and the wage earners or G.I.s who gambled their small savings in the hope of making a quick, gratuitous profit. It was a case of thousands of people betting their life's savings on invisible horses running at a nonexistent track. In fact, even the men taking the people's money could not be seen.

This is how it worked. The coxey would open an account by calling the victim long distance. He would frequently announce that he was phoning from Wall Street, a fact which had a strong impact due to the surging market in legitimate securities. After making a number of wild claims about the watered stock he was selling, he would plead, "Mr. Jones, just make a small purchase in this stock so that we can demonstrate what we can do for you."

Mr. Jones, ordinarily a reasonable man, might be a little suspicious. So he would inquire how the stock salesman had obtained his name. "You are a well-known, respected member of your community," the coxey would reply. "One of our clients in your town recommended you. Of course, I can't tell you who he is. Not allowed to give out names."

At this point the customer might take his first nibble, already having been conditioned by a "send out" or a pamphlet mailed to his home which touted the potential riches of the stock issue being sold. His initial investment, fifty to one hundred dollars. The next step was to separate the victim from his retirement savings, car, home or whatever could be turned into cash. This part of the operation required the services of a real pro, the loader.

The loader sought out such information as the blue chips already owned by the victim, the sums he had hidden away in his bank account, indeed, every penny he could possibly raise by putting his family, relatives, friends and himself into hock. Once armed with this information, the loader would attempt to sell ever greater quantities of nearly worthless stock, frequently switching the customer out of such blue chips as General Motors or A.T. & T.

After the loaders came the superloaders or dynamiters, the highest paid and most expert con men in the hierarchy of boiler-room salesmen. Their boast was that they could pry loose all the customers' cash or assets, force their victims to go into debt and even steal from the church Sunday School fund. Such were the talents the dynamiters displayed, that they frequently managed to make their victims do just that.

Typical of the dynamiter and his wiles was the salesman who acquired the nickname "The Flapper." Before phoning a prospective customer, he would turn himself into a human windmill by vigorously waving his arms. Then, his voice throbbing with the appropriate quality of breathless enthusiasm, he would phone his victims and relate what he "just learned on the floor" or "just picked up in a board room." He was surpassed, if such is possible, by a group of salesmen who had acquired a list of all the ordained Lutheran ministers in the United States. Though these loaders happened to belong to other faiths, it did not deter them from introducing themselves to the ministers they were about to swindle as distant cousins or nephews several times removed.

The rewards for this type of activity astounded even the more sophisticated S.E.C. investigators. One sales manager was able to draw $150,000 in commissions from management of a single boiler room and $75,000 went to a loader who pocketed the sum for only six months work. For most of the five hundred ex-carnival hucksters and siding salesmen, it proved the opportunity of a larcenous lifetime.

The S.E.C. investigators soon discovered that however

great the winnings that fell into the hands of the coxeys, loaders and dynamiters, the salesmen were only minor players in a larger drama. The major roles belonged to the most skilled swindlers, the promoters and boiler-room organizers. While operating in the background, they were to garner millions in illicit profits for their even more shadowy backers. What follows is the story about one of the principal boiler-room promoters used by organized crime in its invasion of Wall Street. It is the tale of Stanley Ira Younger, a man of unusual talents.

Younger, dark, handsome, and apparently quick to learn, began his career as a securities salesman for a Canadian brokerage house. By the time he was twenty-eight, he had prepared for his first solo venture. It consisted of the formation of Provincial American Securities, Inc., which was duly registered with the S.E.C. in May, 1956, as a broker-dealer and began immediately to boiler-room stock out of a Wall Street address.*

That fall it was raided by the New York office and an investigation was launched into possible criminal violations. Since it takes time to develop such information, Windels, as a stopgap measure, ordered his staff to close the firm on bookkeeping and other technical violations. Shortly thereafter the Commission obtained a permanent injunction against the firm. Although Younger insisted he was no longer in the securities business, the New York State Attorney General's office found Provincial American still operating. In August, 1957, another injunction was obtained against Younger, permanently forbidding him to sell stocks in New York State.

---

* Younger was able to register because at that time he had no record of securities violations.

The stock promoter, however, had only begun to operate. According to the New York State Attorney General's office, it wasn't long before Younger became allied with organized crime. As the result of the swindles which were to follow, the investing public lost at least three million dollars through the purchase of three securities issues in which the underworld showed more than a passing interest.

The cast of characters who were to figure prominently in these ventures included:

Carmine Lombardozzi. The reported backer of the underworld's invasion of The Street. A Brooklyn gangster, Lombardozzi is also dark, good-looking, with the physique of a stevedore. He received his earlier schooling among the loan sharks that infested New York's waterfront and in the juke-box rackets. The latter almost cost him his life. He was one of a number of assorted underworld characters who attended the gathering at Apalachin, New York, in November, 1957. Lombardozzi, according to Lt. James S. Mooney, had been forced to wait in host Joseph Barbara's garage while a court of his peers debated a gangland death sentence on charges relating to the juke-box industry. In testimony before the Senate Rackets Committee, the New York policeman added that the sentence was changed to a $10,000 fine. As the power behind the infiltration of Wall Street, Lombardozzi was a shadowy figure who rarely if ever appeared at the boiler-room offices. He usually could be reached at his unlikely headquarters, a Fifth Avenue dress shop.

Arthur Tortorello. Lombardozzi's chief henchman, Tortorello's worldly attainments included a robust record of burglary and grand larceny convictions. If you wanted to meet Lombardozzi, you first talked to Tortorello.

Louis Michael DeFilippo. On a lower rung, DeFilippo,

like Tortorello, was a man of limited but brutish talents. He also possessed a criminal record including a conviction for robbery, several parole violations and arrests for conspiracy and burglary. DeFilippo served as a dummy stockholder, pot watcher and loader.

Murray Taylor. Younger's sales manager, Taylor was charged with seeing that the boiler room's daily operations ran smoothly. A man of varied talents, Taylor, alias Murray Bleefield, had been convicted of arson, subornation of perjury and at one time had served two years in prison on a charge in connection with the Lindbergh kidnaping.

This then was the crew that found the securities markets of the late 1950's promising a harvest as easy to gather as the one that endowed the underworld beer barons of the 1920's. But in contrast to the brawn employed in the sale of illicit hops, the merchandising of watered stock called for an uncommon amount of brains and skill. It needed someone like Stanley Younger who knew his way around the complicated securities laws.

The meeting between Younger and the "mob" apparently took place shortly after the closing of Provincial American in the summer of 1957. The stock promoter, badly in need of funds, was reportedly forced to borrow a large sum, estimated as high as $300,000. Allegedly the underworld extended the money. Just how the take over was supposed to have occurred was fully described in an affidavit filed in New York State Supreme Court by Carl Madonick, head of the Securities Fraud Section of the New York State Attorney General's office:

According to statements made to the Attorney General's office, Stanley I. Younger at the beginning of January, 1958, became severely indebted to persons who made substantial loans of money to him. The financial creditors of Younger at this time appeared to be pressing for payment. Because of the pressure able to be mustered by these creditors, Younger sought feverishly for funds to establish a new securities house. These funds were provided by elements of the Brooklyn mob, reported to include Carmine Lombardozzi and his lieutenants, in return for virtual control of Younger's securities firm.

It was at this time that evidence of strong-arm activities became apparent. The funds received by Younger from the Brooklyn mob were used to finance the operations of another securities firm established by Younger, Alan Russell Securities, Inc. This firm was permanently enjoined from the securities business on application of the Attorney General of the State of New York because of its notorious boiler-room activities.

Younger was then forced to look for more fertile fields because of his intensified obligations to the Brooklyn mob. Younger and his gangster backers muscled into the operations of an established over-the-counter securities house, Lincoln Securities Corporation of 42 Broadway, New York City, New York.

Throughout the machinations of Younger, the man used for the "inside position" was Murray Taylor. Murray Taylor was placed in charge of the salesmen of Lincoln Securities Corp. as their sales manager. It was Murray Taylor, a convicted conspirator, who thereafter took complete charge of Lincoln Securities Corp. arranging for the opening and maintenance of bank accounts, discounting checks, the hiring and firing of sales personnel and the manner of sale of securities by Lincoln Securities Corp.

The operations of Lincoln Securities Corp. were so much within the control of gangster elements that the firm received confirmations for sales of stock not even made from its offices at 42 Broadway but from several uptown offices staffed by persons not recorded on the books and records of Lincoln Securities Corp. as employees and placed in these offices by members of the mob. It was through the maneuvering by these mobsters in their use of Lincoln Securities that the Attorney General of this state was able to crack the surface legitimacy that was attempted to be installed to cover these transactions by the Brooklyn mob.

Lincoln Securities and the stock it sold were typical of Younger's and the underworld's operations. They also illustrated how a clever promoter managed to cloak the origin and sources of an illegal securities distribution. For the underworld this exercise in flimflam netted hundreds of thousands of dollars in profits. For the gullible and eager investors it meant over a half-million dollars loss.

Lincoln Securities was organized as a broker-dealer firm in the fall of 1953 by Lester Ober, a stock salesman from Beverly Hills, California. For the first five years, the firm specialized in highly speculative oil, gas and uranium securities. These securities are known as "sex appeal" stocks because they appear highly attractive, are frequently volatile and often bring the hungry investor a serious amount of trouble. Apparently the securities Ober sold had more than their share of "sex appeal." Over the years, officials in five different states issued a series of orders demanding that Lincoln cease peddling much of its stock.

In the beginning of 1958, Lester Ober found himself facing a more urgent problem. Arthur Tortorello, Lombardozzi's henchman, had become a director of the brokerage house. At about the same time Murray Taylor, convicted conspirator, took over as sales manager. For Lester Ober, who continued as president, the control of Lincoln Securities had passed out of his hands.

The scene now shifts to Canada and a company named Shoreland Mines. Shoreland Mines typifies the company sought by boiler-room promoters. The firm was originally incorporated under the name of Shoreland Gold Mines, Ltd., in the Province of Ontario shortly after the end of World War II. Some eight years later the name was changed to Shoreland Mines Limited, the word "Gold" being dropped. Later attempts to develop mining properties in Quebec proved unsuccessful. By 1958, Shoreland Mines Limited was little more than a corporate shell with hardly any assets. Though nearly worthless the company's stock was to prove the ideal merchandise for Younger and the boiler room salesmen.

In February, 1958, Younger arranged through a Canadian associate to purchase 500,000 control shares of Shoreland Mines Limited from the owner of the company. The price Younger paid was $30,000 or 16 2/3 cents per share. At no time during 1958 were Shoreland's assets worth more than $1,600. It would appear that Younger had just thrown away a considerable sum of money. But appearances are deceiving. Actually, the promoter had taken the first necessary step in the subsequent swindle.

Within a month after he had acquired the control shares, Younger arranged for an organizational meeting and election of officers. Needless to say, Younger's own name did not appear on the list of candidates.

Shoreland, however, neither controlled nor owned any property. This meant that as a mining company its stock was actually worthless. As we shall see, Younger was going to make it appear that this corporation had thousands of dollars worth of assets.

The promoter now proceeded to carry out the following two-pronged plan: (1) Make it appear that Shoreland stock was valuable by having Shoreland acquire thousands of dollars worth of mining property. (The property proved nearly worthless at the time, but the public was never told this.) (2) Hide Younger's identity as the owner of Shoreland Mines stock and at the same time transfer the stock from Canada into the United States.

To carry out the first part of his plan, Younger acquired options on fifty mining claims in Mt. Wright, Quebec, an area purportedly rich in iron ore.* Next he transferred the mining options to Shoreland which paid a one dollar token fee. As a result of this maneuver, when the time came to sell the stock to the public the boiler-room salesmen could claim that Shoreland was in a position to develop a potentially rich mining area. As we shall soon see such claims were to prove more fancy than fact.

Younger was then ready for the second part of his plan —to conceal the true ownership of the 500,000 control shares he had purchased. At the same time the promoter had to bring those securities from Canada to the boiler room in New York. In doing so, he also had to make it appear that an eager market existed for the stock.

He managed to cloak his original purchase by passing the stock through a chain of dummies or associates and brokers before it was handed over to Lincoln Securities. The description of the following maneuvers typifies the manipulations that precede the boiler-rooming of stock.

To disguise the source of the securities, Younger had several associates open trading accounts with a number of Canadian brokers. Among those participating in this part of the scheme were Linda Lord, alias Vicky Leinen, a redhead

* Younger had promised to pay $10,000 for the mining options. The promoter, however, saved himself this sum by forgetting his promise.

of specific accomplishments who served as Younger's girl friend, and Louis DeFilippo.

The first step was to have Miss Lord, DeFilippo and others sell over 400,000 shares of Younger's Shoreland Mines stock to a group of Canadian brokers. Though Younger had paid about 16 cents a share for Shoreland's nearly worthless stock, the Canadian brokers bought the shares at from 70 cents to $1.50 a share. The Canadian brokers were willing to pay these highly inflated prices because Lincoln Securities, the American brokerage house controlled by Younger and the underworld, had already arranged to buy the Shoreland stock from the Canadian firms. In turn, Lincoln Securities completed the last link in the chain by selling the stock to the public for as much as two dollars per share. Younger, of course, never bothered to register the sale of the issue with the S.E.C., an understandable oversight.

This then is what Younger had accomplished: (1) He had managed to hide the origin of the stock by passing it through a group of associates and their dummy accounts, who, in turn, sold it to Canadian brokers who finally placed it in the hands of the boiler-room salesmen. And (2) The money the American public had paid for this stock had been passed backwards through the same people who had funneled the securities from Canada into the United States.

As a result of these slight-of-hand operations in two countries nearly two thousand innocent people were cleaned out of more than $500,000.

We can now describe just how this worthless stock was sold to "investors." The actual boiler-rooming of Shoreland Mines securities in the United States began in April, only two months after Younger had purchased the 500,000 control shares. In fact, the initial sales started before Murray Taylor, the sales manager at Lincoln, was prepared to do business. While Taylor busied himself enlarging his staff of con men, long-distance telephone calls began emanating from the apartment of Linda Lord, located at 11 Fifth Avenue, the gateway to Washington Square and Greenwich Village. Within one month, salesmen using Linda Lord's phone ran up toll charges totaling eight hundred dollars, of which three hundred were eventually paid by Younger.

Meanwhile, Taylor had managed to hire nearly a dozen coxeys, loaders and dynamiters who had previously worked with him during the operation of another boiler room. During this hiatus, a clerical staff mailed thousands of pieces of literature describing the potentials of Canadian ore and mining securities.

Following the deluge of sales literature, Lincoln's salesmen began calling the victims who had responded to the mailed pieces, pressuring them into buying Shoreland Mines securities. Among their more fantastic claims was the representation that the Mt. Wright property on which Shoreland (through Younger) had taken an option was separated by a "wire fence" from a producing mine owned by United States Steel Corporation. They would then volunteer the claim that a vein of iron ore from U. S. Steel's property ran into the area controlled by Shoreland.

The truth, of course, was that U. S. Steel owned no property in the area. Shoreland's so-called Mt. Wright claims were located 200 to 300 miles from the nearest railroad and the only way to reach the property was to attempt to land a plane in the area, a hazardous venture that made any form of commercial production impossible.

Other spurious claims included promised stock splits, that Shoreland could only go up in value, that the mining firm would pay good dividends and that the company was in sound financial condition. One Texas purchaser, who had been induced into buying 700 shares, declared in an affidavit he had been told ". . . some Canadian company had put up $2,000,000 to buy a controlling interest at $2.60 per share and this would be consummated on or before the middle of August and from this they could get me enough money to pay for all my investment with a profit." He also said he had been told the stock would go up to five to ten dollars a share, that Shoreland's property was bordered on either side by U. S. Steel and Jones and Laughlin and finally that Shoreland's "property has had a magnetic survey that says it has a higher content of iron ore than that on either side of it."

Between April 10 and August 15, a period of four months, Lincoln's salesmen were to distribute over 400,000 shares* of Shoreland to customers in forty states, the Panama Canal Zone and Argentina. The prices paid for these shares were arbitrarily raised from 95 cents to $2 a share. How lucrative such an operation can be may be gleaned from the following. During a period of less than three weeks, 335 customers in thirty-six states bought 176,000 shares, paying over $275,-000. Besides salesmen's commissions, postage and printing, the boiler room's heaviest expense was the long distance phone calls which amounted to about $7,000 a month. With such immense profits and comparatively small costs, it was no

---

* The purveyors of Shoreland Mines stock also attempted thousands of "wooden sales." A "wooden sale" is a device whereby confirmation of an order is sent to a customer even though he did not agree to purchase the stock. The boiler-room loader hopes that the victim will pay for the shares instead of arguing with the salesman.

wonder that the underworld was eager to invade the securities market.

Windels and his S.E.C. investigators had not been idle. As the result of customers' complaints and an investigation, the S.E.C. sent its lawyers into court to seek a temporary restraining order that would stop the sale of Shoreland Mines stock. The S.E.C. sought the court order on June 25. It was issued by the U. S. District Court that same day against Younger, Ober, Taylor and their salesmen.

Some of the salesmen at Lincoln Securities simply ignored the court order and continued to sell Shoreland Mines securities. On July 30 the New York State Department of Law under Attorney General Lefkowitz raided the office and discovered the brokerage firm was still operating as a boiler room.

Meanwhile Younger, facing a barrage of federal and state injunctions and a spreading S.E.C. criminal investigation, fled to Canada. He was accompanied by the peripatetic Louis DeFilippo and a man named Vito Palmeri. Arriving in Toronto on August 25, the youthful promoter subleased an apartment. Not one to while away his time sight-seeing, Younger had two phones installed within twenty-four hours and started once again to boiler-room Shoreland Mines stock to people residing in the United States.

These activities had lasted for a month when Younger and his colleagues were picked up by Toronto detectives on information supplied by the S.E.C. The trio was brought to the Canadian Department of Citizenship and Immigration where they refused to give any information. They were then escorted back to the United States. Though he was to attempt one more fraud, Stanley Younger's days of freedom were numbered.

Despite the more than half-million dollars profit the underworld had made on the Shoreland Mines operation,* the mob continued to press Younger for more money. In desperation Younger resorted to one of the oldest securities frauds. Prevalent before the states began passing the "Blue Sky Laws" (state laws designed to protect the investing public), this swindle literally involved the sale of stock that had no more value than the empty blue sky.

Up to this point, Younger had followed the current fashion in boiler-room fraud which involved the sale of stock of a company that could claim some assets, however meager, several acres of property, a telephone and a few officers. However, to organize even this much of a shell takes time and money, both of which Younger no longer had. Instead, the now bedeviled promoter printed stock certificates and listed on each the impressive-sounding name of National Photocopy, Inc., of Nevada. It was a company that just didn't exist. He then proceeded to dump these certificates on the market and in the process tried to swindle some of the Street's most experienced brokerage houses.

Again Younger's plan was simple. His first stop was a brokerage house in Salt Lake City. There he presented certificates of National Photocopy for sale using the alias of Albert Rubin. Younger managed to get the stocks listed at $10 a share in the wholesale price quotations which are published daily for over-the-counter brokers. By having a quotation listed, Younger had made it appear that a market existed for this nonexistent company's stock.

* On October 6, 1958, the S.E.C. obtained a permanent injunction against Younger, Murray Taylor, Lester Ober and other salesmen as well as Lincoln Securities. This injunction was obtained upon the consent of Younger and others after a hearing before Federal Judge Bryan in the U. S. District Court for the Southern District of New York.

He then returned to Wall Street and commenced trading in the imaginary securities. He began by visiting some of the established brokerage houses. A man of many aliases, Stanley Younger, who in a moment of rare wit once traveled as Dr. Livingston, assumed the name of his former father-in-law, Abraham Jacobs, a successful businessman. Using the name of Jacobs without his father-in-law's knowledge or permission, Younger attempted to open accounts at eight leading brokerage houses. He then placed orders with these houses to buy shares of National Photocopy for his account. At the same time he put in sell orders for selected blue chip stocks which, of course, he didn't own.

Younger figured the scheme would not be exposed immediately since under the Street's rules he had at least three days in which to hand over the blue chip certificates to the brokerage houses. The brokers, meanwhile, were told that the proceeds from the (nonexistent) blue chip stocks would pay for the National Photocopy shares. All Younger had to do was to wait while the money from the sale of the phantom blue chip stocks rolled into his fictitious account in Salt Lake City, which was the only source of supply for the nonexistent National Photocopy shares.

Though at least one brokerage house was to lose $5,000 as the result of this scheme, several became suspicious. The hoax was exposed following an inquiry by a broker at the S.E.C.'s New York office. He was shown Younger's photo and the promoter's identification immediately followed. On November 1, 1960, Stanley Younger pleaded guilty in Federal Court to a variety of charges involving National Photocopy.* A short time later he was sentenced to three and a half years

* National Photocopy is not to be confused with American Photocopy Equipment Company, a legitimate firm listed on the New York Stock Exchange.

in prison. It was one of the quickest stock fraud prosecutions on record thanks to the efforts of Jerome J. Londin, then Executive Assistant U. S. Attorney for the Southern District of New York. National Photocopy was Younger's last scheme. As a consequence of his earlier boiler-room activities and the work of the S.E.C.'s Special Investigations Unit, Younger has been indicted on criminal charges by Federal grand juries in Cleveland, Ohio, New Haven, Connecticut, and Concord, New Hampshire.

The New Haven indictment involved forty-seven people and was one of the largest stock fraud cases ever instigated by the S.E.C. Among those indicted were the underworld figures Carmine Lombardozzi, Arthur Tortorello, Louis De-Filippo and Murray Taylor. The indictment covered the fraudulent sale of Atlas Gypsum, a swindle that cost the public an estimated two million dollars. For his role in this boiler-room operation, Younger, who pleaded guilty to mail fraud and violation of the S.E.C.'s regulations, was sentenced to eight years at the Federal correction institution in Danbury, Connecticut. This sentence will begin after he completes his three and a half year jail term in the National Photocopy fraud. He will also serve a three year concurrent sentence growing out of the Concord indictment involving a $750,000 boiler-room swindle in Monarch Asbestos, also a Canadian issue. In addition, Younger received a two-year concurrent sentence in connection with Shoreland Mines.*

---

* Among those indicted in Cleveland in connection with the Lincoln Securities' Shoreland Mines case were Tortorello, DeFilippo, Vito Palmeri, Murray Taylor, Lester Ober and Linda Lord. Both Tortorello and DeFilippo pleaded guilty in connection with Shoreland Mines to charges of violating the antifraud provisions of the 1933 Securities Act. They were sentenced to three years in jail, the sentences to be suspended after they had served three months.

Despite the new safeguards and the recent law-enforcement accomplishments of the S.E.C. and the New York State Attorney General's office, one must ask a vital question: Can the underworld's invasion of Wall Street occur again? The answer is an unqualified yes. Such an invasion, however, would have to overcome a number of difficulties.

The rise of the boiler room era of the 1950's was in part a result of a booming stock market and the accompanying feverish speculation of thousands of small investors. Until the bubble burst in the spring of 1962 the fever reached a new height. Financial writer Richard Phalon of *The New York Herald Tribune* noted in his series on "The Bull Market—1961" that between November, 1960, and April, 1961, the over-the-counter stock averages have been rising almost twice as fast as the Dow-Jones industrials. He added:

"The averages don't tell the whole story. The big speculative surge has been in low-priced 'science' stocks. Almost any issue with a Buck Rogerish tinge to its name was bound to go into orbit. A thousand dollars put into a random selection of twenty-five such stocks three months ago, for instance, would now be worth $1,475 and there seems to be some justification for the widespread conviction among Wall Streeters that many 'new wave' happy investors are indeed buying the way a casual two-dollar bettor picks a horse—purely on the basis of name, with no reference to form or fundamentals."

They were also placed on five years probation. These sentences were to run concurrently with identical sentences given out as the result of guilty pleas made by Tortorello and DeFilippo in connection with the boiler-rooming of Atlas Gypsum. Carmine Lombardozzi, who pleaded nolo contendere or no contest in connection with Atlas Gypsum, received a three year suspended sentence, was placed on five years probation and fined $2,500. The net result: Tortorello and DeFilippo will each serve three months in jail and Lombardozzi will have to pay a $2,500 fine with no jail sentence.

The speculative atmosphere that Richard Phalon discussed is only a repetition of the uranium and mining boom of the past decade, then accompanied by the volcanic upsurge in boiler-room activity. It was an era when the small investor not only bought long with a short memory, having forgotten the lessons of the twenties, but a time when he again proved in numerous instances that his gullibility could not be impaired. His losses as a result of the uranium boom alone during a two year period—from 1953 to 1955—have been estimated at $125 millions. Interestingly, more than five hundred uranium companies born during that two-year period and in which the public so heavily invested have since gone out of business.*

As we move from decade to decade it appears that the times are often opportune for the resurgence of boiler rooms. The stock market that continues to soar, the presence of a large number of unsophisticated investors, the sweepstake mentality of making a fortune while one sleeps, the willingness, indeed the eagerness with which the con men's sales pitch is accepted, all these factors are still with us and make us ripe for the loaders' and dynamiters' plucking. It is in such an atmosphere that the underworld can thrive.

The problem is further complicated by the lack of official notice and action in the neglected danger that organized crime poses. We are, of course, constantly reminded of the obvious criminal acts. As a source of headlines and mass titillation the blood and mayhem of the underworld has had few equals. However, a more insidious activity is too rarely

* This does not mean that the uranium boom itself was basically fraudulent. Most companies represented in a straightforward way that they had no uranium and that the odds were against their finding it, which meant the investor would lose what he put in. On the other hand if they did discover uranium ore, a few dollars investment could become quite valuable.

explored, the attempt by organized crime to encroach on legitimate business.

The reasons for this attempted infiltration follow a logical pattern. The syndicates, born during the bootlegging era of the twenties, are still in existence, though their organizational make-up has changed and nearly all of their personnel have been replaced. Their main aim, then as now, is to enlarge their financial holdings. Though the sources of the underworld's funds may be gambling, narcotics and prostitution, organized crime constantly seeks new enterprises where with a minimum of risk it can make profitable investments. What is most important, the underworld possesses the necessary venture capital, that is large cash reserves or assets that can be quickly turned into cash. With the times propitious, it was not surprising that organized crime sought profits in securities.

Further, as a business investment boiler rooms need a large initial cash outlay to get started. It is estimated that a boiler-room promoter to begin operations may have to have on hand as much as $200,000. This large sum includes money spent on the original purchase of the stock to be sold or in organizing the corporate shell and acquiring some assets, passing the fraudulent shares through brokers, the acquisition of "sucker" lists, heavy mailings of promotional material, initial commissions to salesmen, lawyers' fees and finally those long-distance telephone tolls. The S.E.C. discovered one boiler room had actually run up a $200,000 phone bill in a six-month period, a record of its kind. The underworld with its large cash resources can easily afford such undertakings.

There is, though, a decided difference between the way organized criminal elements run such ventures and the manner in which swindlers not affiliated with the underworld operate. "Several boiler-room salesmen told me," Windels recalled, "what it was like before the mobsters took over. The deals then were about fifty per cent legitimate. After the underworld's arrival the operation became a one hundred per cent swindle.

"There was another difference," he went on. "This was in the area of their own enforcement problems. Whenever a dispute arose over methods of operation or profits the underworld couldn't very well take it to court. The whole scheme would be exposed. It was not uncommon for such disputes to be adjudicated by underworld figures and lawyers, the final decisions being strictly enforced.

"In one instance a difference of opinion arose over a certain bundle of stock that was to come out of Canada into the U.S. The market in the stock was to be rigged and the stock to be sold through a boiler room. A dispute arose over the price at which the securities were to be sold to the boiler room and the methods of payment. A meeting was held in Canada and included criminal figures from the east and middle west. The presiding officer was an underworld lawyer. He judiciously settled the dispute and the stock was sold to the unsuspecting public."

In addition to the continued speculative surge among a number of uninformed people and the resources in the hands of shady promoters, there is another factor that would make it possible for organized crime to invade Wall Street again. One of the most telling advantages given to the securities swindler is mystery, the mother of manipulation. In the hide-and-seek game of stock chicanery, mystery, when shrewdly utilized, has made it possible for some swindlers to bilk the public and yet remain practically immune to legal action.

One of the most troublesome problems the S.E.C. and others face in dealing with the unscrupulous promoter is his ability to cloak his manipulations through the employment of foreign sources. The extent of the problem may be measured by the following figures of securities sold by broker-dealer firms located in the New York regional area between 1955 and 1956. During that period over thirty-eight million shares of heavily watered and nearly worthless stock were dumped on the public. These shares, representing fifty-four separate mining, oil and other highly speculative ventures involved Canadian issuers or securities of American issuers originating from Swiss-type trusts or other foreign sources. The total price the public paid for this stock came to over 100 million dollars. By April 22, 1958, the market price had plummeted to seventeen millions. The loss to investors as of that date, $84 million.

One of the largest sources of manipulated stock is the Swiss-type trusts or numbered accounts. In the survey just mentioned, $50 million was spent on stocks emanating from Swiss-type trusts. For the fast-buck promoter a knowledge of how to employ Swiss-type trusts and numbered accounts is often mandatory. Such knowledge may facilitate the eventual promotion of securities. But more important, it is often essential for hiding the names of the promoter himself and his underworld backers. For Federal and state investigators, however, the problems posed by foreign bank accounts in cloaking the origin of a securities swindle are often impossible to solve.

How this problem came about has an interesting history,

which originally was in no way connected with euchring the Iowa widow out of her life savings. Unlike the banking practices in the United States, it is the custom among such institutions in most European countries to deny access to any information in its books or files to foreign government agencies. The Swiss, however, went a step further. In 1934, they passed a series of laws which prohibit Swiss banks from disclosing such institutions' secrets including the identity of individuals for whom the bank may be acting. The laws specifically prohibit the disclosure of such information to foreign government agencies. The purpose of these laws was to safeguard the assets entrusted to Swiss banks by residents of other countries overrun by fascists or communists.

To hide a customer's identity and thus prevent confiscation of his savings by his own government, a Swiss bank may set up what is known as a numbered account. After giving a bank executive his name, occupation and nationality, the customer, if he chooses, may receive a number which is the sole means of identification of his account. Also, if he desires, all correspondence from the bank will be sent on plain stationery and mailed by a bank employee in the customer's country.

Numbered accounts and Swiss trusts proved helpful not only to refugees of tyranny but tyrants themselves, including, reportedly, several deposed South American dictators. They also have been used by securities swindlers and manipulators to mask their true identity, and at the same time avoid registration under the Securities laws. By means of such a trust the stock can be sold to the public without a statement informing the buyer of the actual worth of the company and its shares.

The employment of Swiss-type trusts—they can also be

found in Liechtenstein and North African banks—and Canadian sources were the basic weapons used by the boiler-room promoters who followed Tellier. Unlike Tellier, who submitted offering circulars and other material to the S.E.C. under the Regulation A exemption, the promoters who succeeded him rarely registered the issues they sold with the Commission. To protect themselves from prosecution for failure to comply with the S.E.C.'s registration requirements, these promoters—Younger was a typical example—would originate the stock issue in Canada and then conceal the true ownership of the securities by passing them through dummy accounts located in Canadian brokerage houses.

Boiler-room promoters employed Swiss-type trusts for the same reasons. The only difference was that the securities funneled through the anonymous numbered accounts first originated in the United States instead of Canada. The Swiss-type trusts not only allowed the promoters to mask the true ownership of the securities but also served as a means of cloaking the origin of the money used to manipulate the market and pay off the so-called investment advisers. Finally, since the S.E.C. cannot examine the records of a Swiss-type trust, the promoters in many instances were and still are able to avoid exposure and prosecution.

How a group of promoters employed a Swiss-type trust to boiler-room securities was brought out in testimony before the Internal Security subcommittee of the United States Senate. This particular scheme cost the investing public over $6,500,000. The witness testifying is Paul Windels, Jr.

The first example I would like to give you involves an American corporation which is engaged in looking for and drilling for oil. This corporation had need for additional financing. It wanted approximately a million dollars and had outstanding

250,000 shares of stock held by various existing stockholders. It went to a Swiss trust and the Swiss trust, for $1,300,000, purchased [an additional] 750,000 shares of the stock [supposedly for investment purposes]. . . . In this particular case the shares were sold almost immediately, commencing within a matter of two or three days and having been purchased for one to three dollars a share [by U.S. promoters from the Swiss trust], they were sold to the American public at between ten and twelve dollars a share. The value of the stock has since fallen to below the price paid by the Swiss trust, so you can appreciate the extent of the loss, and also the extent of the profit to the insiders on that transaction.

ROBERT MORRIS (*Committee Counsel*): In this case there is no way to ascertain at that point, by either your agency or the United States Government, as to precisely who it was that made the money?

WINDELS: That's right. And of course we particularly are not able to connect by evidence the management of the corporation with the public distribution.

Despite the employment of Swiss-type trusts, the cash resources of the underworld and a gullible public, the boiler-room promoters should certainly find life more complicated during the 1960's. This improved state of affairs for the investor can be attributed in large part to tighter securities regulations and crime-busting techniques worked out by Windels and the New York Regional Office in conjunction with the Special Investigations Unit and the S.E.C.'s General Counsel's office. These techniques, I might add, were largely responsible for driving the underworld from Wall Street and ending the boiler-room era of the fifties.

"Our first big problem," Windels explained, "was time. It was obvious from the outset that the more than two hundred boiler-room operations we eventually raided were participating in a series of gigantic frauds. But gathering evidence that proves a swindle takes time. And that was one thing we didn't have. For every day these boiler rooms continued to operate the investing public was losing a fortune. For us the big questions were—how to knock the boiler rooms out of action, do it quickly, and still follow the judicial procedure embodied in the Securities laws that Congress passed. We managed all these things by employing what for these purposes may be called a technicality under the law."

The technicality Windels referred to is known as the net capital rule, a provision promulgated by the S.E.C. This rule provides that a broker-dealer must have cash assets which exceed all of his liabilities except liabilities adequately secured by other collateral. The purpose is to make sure that the broker-dealer will always have enough cash or other liquid assets so that he can pay his customers' claims whenever they make them.

Windels continued: "As soon as we took one look at the boiler-rooms' operations, I realized we had them in a bind. All we had to do was apply the net capital rule. It worked this way. To insure a maximum profit from their own swindle, the boiler-room operators had delayed delivery of thousands of dollars worth of stock they had already sold to customers over the phone. The lag in delivery ran from several weeks to a couple of months. The delays prevented the victims from selling the stock back to the promoters while they were busy manipulating the market and raising the price of the stock. In other words, by not immediately delivering the securities the boiler-room operators would not be forced by the victims to do what the Street calls 'eat' their own stock at higher prices. Of course, this meant that since the boiler-room operators still owed thousands of dollars worth of shares to their customers their liabilities were greater than their assets. The result, massive violations of the net capital rule. Thus, by utilizing a technicality in the regulations we were able to close down immediately most of the boiler rooms we raided."

An additional weapon were the raids themselves. It was the first time in the history of the S.E.C. that so many simultaneous visitations in force had been carried out. The S.E.C. raiders, however, were not the only ones taking action. The New York State Attorney General's office, acting under the state's Blue Sky laws, also cracked down on a number of boiler rooms, and obtained State Supreme Court injunctions permanently forbidding the operators to sell securities in New York.

Though the Federal and New York State raids often proved effective, the Commission's law-enforcement officers had only begun their task. The S.E.C. frequently discovered that while closing down one boiler room, the same men would form another house to sell still another issue of worthless securities. To put this hard core of con men and promoters out of business called for stiffer penalties. "The final weapon, and the one that is most effective," Windels declared, "is criminal action. Criminal action can mean jail sentences, and that's when we really get results."

But obtaining criminal convictions can take time. When full legal action is brought by the Federal government it usually follows a two-step process, first civil, then criminal. In instances involving securities violations, the S.E.C. attorneys handle only the civil procedure. This means the S.E.C. lawyers can go into court and, if they prove their case, obtain civil injunctions which prohibit a boiler-room operator from selling a particular stock in a fraudulent manner. No jail penalties are involved unless the swindler defies the court injunction. In fact, all the promoter needs to do is to stop selling securities in a crooked fashion. He will still be able to pocket his ill-gotten gains for which he will be neither jailed nor fined.

Before a swindler can be put behind bars, the S.E.C. must first collect the evidence for a criminal prosecution, then hand the case over to one of the Justice Department's Attorneys for action. All this can be time consuming.

In the case of the boiler rooms, Windels and his S.E.C. investigators were faced with still another problem. How to prove that a criminal fraud had actually taken place? The boiler-room operators had relied on one basic instrument to sell their watered and nearly worthless stock, the telephone. Though the coxeys, loaders and dynamiters had lied, cheated and conned their victims over the phone, the S.E.C. faced the very difficult task of proving that the calls had been made from a specific boiler room and, most important, identify the salesmen who had made the calls.

In almost every instance the victims had never seen the salesmen who had swindled them. The phone calls originated from boiler rooms located hundreds to thousands of miles away. Thus, it appeared that the only identification the victims could hope to make was the sound of the salesman's voice, hardly evidence worthy enough to obtain a criminal conviction in a complex million-dollar securities swindle. Finally, the S.E.C. had to gather enough evidence for dozens of swindles involving thousands of victims.

The backbone of the S.E.C.'s effort to collect this evidence was a four-page questionnaire compiled by Bill Moran and the New York staff. The questionnaire, to be sent to boiler-room victims, had to be lengthy enough so that the S.E.C. could obtain the necessary information. At the same time it could not be so technical that the ordinary stock purchaser would be incapable or unwilling to fill it out. In addition, under the provisions of the Securities laws the S.E.C. is prohibited from judging the quality of a stock issue. This meant the questions could not reflect on the worth or worthiness of the securities being investigated.

The questionnaire, divided into sixteen sections, posed thirty-seven questions, most of them of the "Yes" or "No" variety. So far over fifty thousand questionnaires have been mailed to victims. The victims' names were obtained as a result of the massive raids conducted by the New York staff.

The questionnaire the S.E.C. sent out seemed innocuous. Among the questions posed: When and by what means was your attention first called to the stock of the subject company? By what securities firm, salesman or individual? What, if any, telephone statements induced you to purchase stock of the subject company? Did you receive a descriptive pamphlet or other sales literature on the above subject company? Was such material delivered to you by mail?

Noncommittal, simple fact-finding questions. Nothing dramatic. But they were to prove deadly.

The ability of the S.E.C. to prepare a criminal case against a boiler-room operator was first shown in the Alaska Telephone trial. Shortly after Paul Windels had been sworn in as Regional Administrator in New York, he was loaned out to the Justice Department as a special prosecuting attorney to handle the Tellier case. Though Tellier personally was in no way connected with the boiler rooms the S.E.C. was investigating, his trial was to set the pattern and precedent for the Commission's and the Justice Department's future action.*

"Perhaps our biggest problem in the Tellier trials was the admission of evidence that a swindle had been perpetrated over the telephone," Windels said. "The pattern we were to use actually proved quite simple. We first showed that many of Tellier's victims had listed their names, addresses and phone numbers on coupons which had been inserted in Tellier-sponsored ads. We also showed that the victims would mail the coupons to Tellier & Co. Then the victims would testify that after they had sent in the coupons to Tellier & Co., they would receive phone calls purportedly from Tellier salesmen who would make their pitch. Presenting the evidence this way, we were able to show that a telephone had been used as the instrument with which the deception had been carried out. Our victory in the battle against the boiler-room operations was assured when the United States Supreme Court declined to review Tellier's conviction."

The S.E.C. did not confine its campaign against boiler rooms with the instigation of criminal action. It has tightened the rules under which securities dealers and brokers must register with the Commission. It not only keeps a surveillance list of new or questionable brokerage operations, but is increasing the number of periodic unannounced inspections of the brokers' salesmen and other personnel, the stocks the house sells and the conditions of the brokers' books.

---

* As the result of the success of the Tellier prosecution, there was a substantial reduction of the effective use of the telephone as a means of concealing the identity of the boiler-room salesmen.

In 1959 the New York State Legislature passed a law on the recommendation of Attorney General Louis J. Lefkowitz that makes it mandatory for all securities salesmen in the State to register with the Attorney General's office. The law requires the salesmen, as well as brokers and dealers, to register every four years and submit a statement detailing their background, experience and any criminal record they may hold. Previously only brokers and dealers (not salesmen) were required to file a dealers' statement. So far, more than thirty thousand securities salesmen in New York have registered.

The possibility remains, however, that even with these law-enforcement advances the boiler-room operators and the organized underworld may yet return to Wall Street.* Despite the periodic warnings issued by the New York Stock Exchange, the S.E.C. and the New York Attorney General's office, the legion of small, always hopeful investors will continue on their speculative way seeking quick fortunes they simply cannot make. Finally, the new manipulative techniques such as Swiss-type trusts make it virtually impossible in some instances for law enforcement agencies to expose many swindles until after thousands of the unsuspecting have been fleeced.

Working for the public are the federal and state agencies whose task is to police the Street. Though they have never been more vigilant, they are often handicapped by a short-

* As recently as January 24, 1962, Robert F. Kennedy, the U. S. Attorney General, said that the Justice Department was investigating reports that gangsters have been planting illicit profits in securities. He added there appeared to have been stepped-up efforts by racketeers in recent years to move into legitimate businesses through the stock market. The Attorney General declined to say at whom the investigation was aimed. He declared, however, there was no evidence to indicate that the major stock exchanges in New York had come under racketeer influence or control.

age of personnel. Their jobs would be made immeasurably easier if the public attempted to protect itself by following these rules prepared by The Better Business Bureau of New York City in cooperation with the S.E.C., the New York State Attorney General's office, and representatives of the stock exchanges and the associations of securities dealers:

1. Think before buying securities.
2. Deal only with a securities firm which you know.
3. Be skeptical of securities offered on the telephone from any firm or salesman you do not know.
4. Guard against all high-pressure sales.
5. Beware of promises of quick spectacular price rises.
6. Be sure you understand the risk of loss as well as the prospect of gain.
7. Get the facts—do not buy on tips or rumors.
8. Request the person offering securities over the phone to mail you written information about the corporation, its operations, net profit, management, financial position, and future prospects. Save all such information for future reference.
9. If you do not understand the written information, consult a person who does.
10. Give at least as much thought when purchasing securities as you would when acquiring any valuable property.

For the Securities and Exchange Commission and Windels the surge of the boiler rooms was only one challenge the agency and the attorney faced. Perhaps the Commission's and Windels' most dramatic case concerned the minister's son who managed single-handedly to outwit some of the nation's shrewdest legal and financial minds. Thereby hangs not only a tale but a fortune in stolen assets and manipulated securities estimated as high as fifty million dollars.

4. THE MASTER MANIPULATOR

When the phone rang shortly after midnight, Paul Windels, Jr., groggily reached for the receiver. The call could not have come at a more trying time. Having just devoted six months to reorganizing the S.E.C.'s New York Regional office, Windels was then spending his days in a Federal courtroom in Brooklyn, conducting the Government's prosecution for the second Tellier trial. The Tellier case, as we saw in Chapter 2, was an intricate, exhausting affair. The second trial eventually filled over four thousand pages with testimony from nearly fifty witnesses.

As a special prosecuting attorney loaned to the Justice Department, Windels tried the case during the day and at night interviewed witnesses in preparation for the following day's testimony. Unknown to many of his colleagues, Windels carried an additional responsibility during those courtroom sessions that were to stretch from January through March, 1957. As we have seen in a previous chapter, the head of the S.E.C.'s New York office was deeply involved in the campaign against boiler rooms. If he expected to attain crim-

inal convictions, he had to create the judicial precedent
and trial pattern for the seemingly most circumscribed type
of evidence, the identification of a swindler over a long-
distance telephone. Windels hoped to create such a precedent in the Brooklyn courthouse by obtaining the underwriter's conviction. The first Tellier trial had ended in a
hung jury. Windels knew that this trial, the second, would be
his last opportunity, not only to convict the king of penny
stocks but to make the pattern of attack on boiler rooms
stick in court. The stakes were high and the attorney's
nerves were drawn to the breaking point.

As the phone rang that February night, Windels lifted the
receiver and sleepily listened to a strange, eager voice. The
voice promised to relate information about a series of massive corporate manipulations. But telling the story would
take time. Would the busy S.E.C. Administrator care to
listen?

The following midnight, after a full day in court and the
evening spent with more witnesses, Windels met his informant in a midtown Manhattan bar. The meeting lasted
until 2 A.M. The same procedure was to take place during
the succeeding three evenings. Windels soon learned his
informant was no ordinary man. A multimillionaire, whose
name to this date has never been revealed, once traveled
all night in an open car through heavy rain to hand personally to the S.E.C. official a document he thought might help
him in his subsequent investigation.

At the nightly meetings the financier would regale Windels with uproarious stories, punctuating his talks by describing a securities swindle so intricate in its design that the
already tired attorney was forced to call on all his mental

resources to comprehend it. As Windels listened, he quickly realized he had the lead that could bring the downfall of this century's most artful financial swindler.

This then is the story of the master of them all, Lowell McAfee Birrell. It is also a tale that touches upon the biggest stock market manipulations since the 1920's. It was the exposure of these manipulations that triggered a Congressional investigation and a full-scale probe of the securities industry by the S.E.C.

Birrell's career began in the grim tradition of the young Horatio Alger. He was born in 1907 in the farming hamlet of Whiteland, Indiana, a community whose population numbered less than a thousand. His early surroundings were severely limited in virtually everything but inspiration, his parents having committed their lives to preaching the gospel. His mother had been a Methodist missionary and his father earned a meager living as an itinerant Presbyterian minister. Restlessly moving from congregation to congregation, the elder Birrell intoned the word of God and somehow managed to clothe, feed and shelter his wife and five children on nine hundred dollars a year. It appears that for Lowell Birrell there always remained the memory of those early days of restless poverty which in the beginning at least served as the catalyst for his ambition.

Birrell's deliverance began in his teens. The magic wand for his escape was his mind, an instrument of extraordinary precocity and brilliance. Syracuse University was to award him a Bachelor's degree at eighteen, the age when most students are first registering for college. He continued at the University of Michigan law school, where his work was sufficiently distinguished to place him on the editorial board of the *Law Review*. He graduated in 1928 near the top of his class.

The year of Birrell's graduation was the climax of an era of frenzied living whose main sources of amusement were smuggled whiskey and an inebriated stock market. However, for Birrell, who later made an avocation of wild times, it was a year of serious endeavor. His first stop was New York City where he simultaneously passed the State Bar examination and obtained a job with the highly reputable Wall Street law firm of Cadwalader, Wickersham & Taft. Birrell was then twenty-one.

As a brilliant corporation counsel, Birrell came to represent E. I. du Pont de Nemours, H. C. Bohack, Bush Terminal, Munson Steamship Lines, and the widow of a former Chairman of the Chase National Bank. He remained with Cadwalader for five years, leaving in 1935 to set up his own office.

It was during this period that Birrell applied his special talents to a series of projects which, if they did not bring him the fantastic returns he later was to expect, gave him invaluable experience in the intricacies of corporate finance. Shortly after the repeal of the Volstead Act, Birrell undertook the reorganization and refinancing of a number of local beer producers, among them Eastern Breweries, Peter Doelger Brewery and Fidelio Brewery, a Brooklyn concern. He acquired control of the latter with the help of the widow of a millionaire cigarette manufacturer. In a series of sleight-of-hand maneuvers he turned Fidelio into a holding company which served as the protective cover and source for many of his later operations. As part of this manipulation Fidelio's name was eventually changed to Greater New York

Industries. Though Birrell certainly had not planned it at the time, Greater New York Industries was to figure in his final and most brilliant machination.

Meanwhile, the budding financier became acquainted with Stewart Hopps, an insurance specialist. Hopps' success in business enabled him to purchase two spacious homes, one of which is located on Belvedere Island overlooking San Francisco Bay. The house—which reportedly cost over $450,000—contains only two bedrooms but has been described by a biographer as "the most expensive four-room home ever built in America." His other home in Palm Springs includes among its trappings a swimming pool with a floating telephone. Although Hopps was Birrell's introduction to the insurance field, he has been able to show in court that if any light-fingered work was done, the hand that did it belonged to Birrell. Added Hopps: "He left me wiser and a good deal poorer."

Typical of the financier's handiwork in general and in the insurance field in particular was his purchase in 1944 of Claude Neon, originally a manufacturer of neon lights. The way Birrell purchased Claude Neon was to have it bought by Greater New York Industries, the brewery-turned-holding company controlled by Birrell. Among Claude Neon's attractions was the possession of $900,000 worth of securities. But by the middle of 1945 these securities, owned by Birrell-dominated Claude Neon, were sold.

This venture, though profitable, was only a minor one for Birrell. Claude Neon was to serve as one of the keys that would allow Birrell to unlock the vaults of a number of insurance companies. The firm's greatest asset was the fact that it was traded on the Curb Exchange, now known as the American Stock Exchange. This meant that Claude Neon's stock had considerable status and thus was easier to exchange for the shares of other companies. Birrell had Claude Neon issue thousands of additional shares which were then used to obtain control of a number of small insurance companies.

Meanwhile, the financier, along with Hopps, had set up a company to manage the investment portfolios of a group of insurance companies. This meant, among other things, that Birrell could select the securities the insurance companies would purchase. His next step was to purchase certain securities at their market value. Then he sold them to Claude Neon, which he controlled, at inflated prices. As investment manager he would then transfer the overvalued securities to the portfolios of the insurance companies who repaid Claude Neon. Thus, Claude Neon was similar to a middle-man buying stocks at inflated prices from Birrell and then selling them to the insurance companies.

The insurance companies began taking on more business on the grounds that the value of their reserves had been increased. This increase, in turn, was based on the injection of the overvalued securities that Birrell had dumped into their holdings. Since Birrell and Hopps were receiving 25 per cent of the insurance companies' net profits as a fee for handling their investments, the increase in the insurance firms' business brought even more profits to them.

The size of the loss to the insurance companies has yet to be fully estimated. An indication of how profitable the operation was can be found in a Federal court order which resulted from a suit brought by Claude Neon. After eleven years of litigation the court ordered Birrell to make restitution of over three and a quarter million dollars to the holding company, the judge declaring "all claims are predicated upon a claim of fraud and I so find."

Toward the end of World War II, when Birrell was making his first inroad on Claude Neon, the financier struck up a friendship with Cecil Parker Stewart. A man of considerable financial interests, Stewart had been told by his doctors that he was an incurable cancer victim and had only six months to live. Only Birrell held out hope, advising Stewart that he knew a Peruvian doctor who possessed a miraculous anti-cancer serum that had already saved one of his friends. Stewart saw the doctor, took the serum and then brought Birrell to his Florida home. As sometimes can happen in incurable cancer cases, the disease may appear to have been miraculously arrested. Stewart, feeling his health had improved, showed his appreciation to Birrell by making him trustee and executor of his estate. Then just as the doctors had predicted, Cecil Parker Stewart died. As executor and trustee, Birrell had gained control of another fortune.

But Birrell was not satiated. Though the acquisition of vast sums apparently was vital to his well-being, there remained an even more tantalizing attraction, devious wheeling and dealing in high corporate finance. Ironically, his brilliant talents exercised in honest endeavor could undoubtedly have given him great wealth, security and prestige. But such activity often lacks the elements that sustain the high-stake players, the thrill of outwitting your opponent, the reward of winner take all. Birrell it appears desired neither fame nor honor as most men have come to know it. What he did crave, though, was ceaseless excitement.

And excitement he had nearly every waking moment of his life. The thrills came in many forms. His days and nights

were a continuous Bacchanalia of whiskey, women and "fun."
Married three times, the master manipulator was frequently
accompanied by beautiful women. A devotee of the café
circuit, he had an immense capacity for liquor, which was
matched only by his recuperative powers. As one acquaintance
noted, "He used to sleep in telephone booths. He'd stay up
at the Copacabana or El Morocco until 3 A.M., drink a lot
and occasionally rest his head against the table or in a telephone booth to catnap. He never closed his eyes for more than
a few minutes. And he never got more than three hours' sleep
a night. But the next morning, before 9 A.M., he'd be back in
his office, bright and alert."

Equally legendary were his phenomenal memory and his
charm, which he used as it suited his purposes. It has been
said that he could read an entire newspaper and then quote
large portions of it verbatim. Years after he read a legal
document he could recall every clause. Needless to say, he
was one of the country's leading experts on the provisions of
the Securities laws.

Though his enemies were understandably numerous, he
had that amazing ability to instill loyalty and friendship
even among some of the people he had hoodwinked. A man
whose company's assets joined Birrell's spoils once declared,
"If he walked in the door now I couldn't hate him, and if he
needed a few hundred bucks he'd get it."

Certainly his greatest social success came with his entrance
among the *haute monde* of Philadelphia society. Birrell's
elevation to the landed gentry began in the forties when he
purchased a 1,000-acre estate near New Hope, in Bucks
County, Pennsylvania. Among its assets were three manor
houses, forty employees, a collection of prize bulls and a
showcase of famous neighbors including Paul Whiteman, the

bandleader, Budd Schulberg, the author, and the late Moss Hart, the playwright. Birrell's bucolic haven also included a pool, a playhouse and a row of slot machines which were conveniently placed at the disposal of his guests. As was to be expected, the slot machines rarely paid off.

Not to be outshone by those who owned yachts, Birrell acquired a forty-foot cruiser which, though it lacked a motor, did possess a bar. There was, however, one hitch. The only place large enough for mooring was the financier's swimming pool. He solved the problem by constructing a seven-acre artificial lake. Unlike its owner, the *Lowell M.B.* never went anywhere, but it did provide his guests with many a liquid voyage as they floated around their convivial host's bar.

It is in this merry setting that we may visualize this son of an Indiana preacher at the height of his success. Carefree but never careless, he would arrive on the weekend after the completion of some complex corporate deal. Immaculately dressed—he favored conservative blue custom-made $250 suits—he would ride down the long private road that led to one of his houses. On the way he might catch a glimpse of the life-sized fire engine his most recent wife bought him for Christmas, or the baby elephant, another present, which he regally fed Scotch. As he arrived at the door he would be greeted by one of his three children or the then current Mrs. Birrell. While he changed into something less formal, a crew of carpenters would be driving the last nails in the stand they had built for that weekend's horse show. Then the guests would begin arriving, sometimes as many as three thousand. They included not only the commoners from the surrounding countryside, but the gentry from the horse and hunt country of nearby Maryland, Delaware,

Virginia and Eastern Pennsylvania. As the festivities got underway, a stranger among the crowd might notice a man of about fifty turning to paunch, his hair thinning, yet his appearance decidedly handsome, his eyes smiling benignly on all that they surveyed. And there would stand the master of Echo Falls Farm. The man who could still remember Whiteland, Indiana, should have at last been satisfied. But Birrell wanted more. And it seemed that it always had to be other people's money that would get it for him.

One government investigator discovered that neither Birrell's charm nor his wealth would ever improve the private image held by some of the financier's neighbors. The investigator recalled how on his way to New Hope he stopped at an inn. "It was an old inn," he said, "but nicely kept up. I asked the bartender if I could see the proprietor. The bartender said he owned the place. It did not take much prodding, though, for him to start talking about his favorite subject, Lowell McAfee Birrell. Birrell had once owned the inn and the bartender had worked there as Birrell's employee. Birrell had used the inn to put up guests. Then one day the financier happened by and asked the bartender if he wanted to buy the place. 'Build the inn up,' Birrell told the bartender. 'But if you can't live up to the mortgage, don't worry about it. I won't press you.' So the bartender invested what was for him a fortune on renovations. The place certainly looked grand. Somehow he managed his first mortgage payment. But when he came to making his second payment, he found he was a little short. He called Birrell and told him that there would be a delay on the second mortgage payment. The financier replied, 'Don't worry about it.' Taking Birrell at his word, the inn's new proprietor didn't worry until the next morning when he received a registered letter demanding that payment be made by three that afternoon or the mortgage would be foreclosed. It was a neat play. If the bartender didn't make the payment, Birrell would have regained the property, completely renovated and improved, at no cost to himself. Fortunately for the bartender he was able to gather together the money and make payment before the deadline."

Birrell, the investigator later learned, was involved in yet another sly deal. Always the perfectionist, the financier decided that he needed to add a neighbor's farm to his estate so that his property would be properly rounded out. The neighbor, a widow, sold her farm to Birrell, or so she thought. Actually Birrell did not pay for the farm in cash. Instead, he handed her a mortgage agreement. Next, he took $5,000 of her husband's life insurance and in return gave her some unregistered Canadian stock which he was then dumping. He then turned around and made his first mortgage payment of $5,000, giving to the widow the money she had given him for the overrated securities. Meanwhile, Birrell had taken title to the property. He buried the title by handing it over to one of his dummy companies. As events would have it, Birrell fled the country without making any further payments on the mortgage. The widow, who wanted to foreclose in order to get her farm back, had the expensive and difficult burden of hiring lawyers to search through the remains of the financier's empire to first find and then repossess the title to her own property.

Birrell, it would appear, had turned his vocation into a hobby. When he was fully occupied, the financier devoted his talents to gutting American corporations. What follows is a description of the financier's take-over and eventual spoiling of a series of legitimate enterprises. The main point to keep in mind, certainly Birrell's aim, was to sell the securities at inflated prices without registering them with the S.E.C., thereby avoiding full disclosure of their actual worth.

The biggest swindle for which Birrell has been indicted begins with the acquisition of two companies completely unrelated in the products they sold. One was Swan-Finch Oil Corporation, which compounded lubricating oil. The other was Doeskin Products, makers of bathroom and facial tissues. As the result of Birrell's manipulations of Swan-Finch Oil and Doeskin he was to be indicted on sixty-nine counts of grand larceny. Birrell himself was to have realized a profit of a minimum of three million dollars. The financier could view his work with considerable pride.

Birrell's acquisition of Swan-Finch was somewhat roundabout though perfectly legitimate. An insurance company, which the financier headed and completely dominated, paid out $250,000 for about 40 per cent of the outstanding Swan-Finch shares. This gave Birrell control. Though the company's sales volume totaled three million a year, it was losing money. It would appear that the financier had not made a very shrewd investment. But with Birrell appearances were invariably deceiving. From the financier's viewpoint Swan-Finch was like the lady of quality who, having fallen upon trying times, still maintained in the eyes of the community an aura of respectability and virtue.

Founded in 1853 as a distributor of sperm oil, Swan-Finch became a part of the old Rockefeller Standard Oil complex. The firm, however, was made to stand on its own feet in 1911 following a government anti-trust action. During the subsequent spin-off, the company ended up in the control of the Moncrieff family, and it was from a later generation of that family that Birrell bought control in 1954.

Also like a lady of quality, Swan-Finch not only had a name that conjured up status but it even had a proper address. For years it had been traded on the Curb Exchange, and then the American Stock Exchange, the second largest exchange in the United States. Though allowed trading privileges on the American Exchange the firm was not actually listed on the exchange. This distinction was important for someone with Birrell's turn of mind. Companies that are fully listed are obliged to publish annual reports as well as other periodic statements showing sales and earnings. In addition controlling persons and corporate officers and directors must publish monthly reports of their own transactions in the securities. Thus, the companies' stockholders and interested members of the public may learn how the firms are doing.

However, unlisted firms like Swan-Finch are allowed trading privileges but are not obliged to publish annual statements.* For Birrell's purposes Swan-Finch was the perfect front for his manipulations. He was not only keeping company with a lady of impeccable reputation and name but could use her as a woman of the streets without anyone except the lady herself knowing the difference. Indeed, she

---

* About one out of five stocks traded on the American Exchange are unlisted. These unlisted privileges were in effect when the Securities Exchange Act of 1934 was passed. Congress simply allowed them to continue. As a result no approval is acquired by the Commission. The unlisted trading privileges which the Commission does approve are those granted to regional exchanges in stocks fully listed elsewhere, which usually means securities listed and currently traded on the New York Stock Exchange. Since they are already fully listed on the Big Board, the companies the securities represent are subject to full reporting and other disclosure requirements. The New York Stock Exchange, incidentally, abolished unlisted trading in 1910.

couldn't even protest, for the master manipulator owned her literally lock, stock and barrel.

No sooner had Birrell gained control of Swan-Finch than he began his campaign to build up the firm's value in the eyes of investors. His method was an old and accepted business practice and is in fact a perfectly legitimate means of corporate expansion. The board of directors of Swan-Finch, which Birrell controlled, simply began issuing new stock which in turn was used for the acquisition of other companies or properties. When the financier took over Swan-Finch in May, 1954, there were 34,793 common shares outstanding. Over the next two and three-quarter years Swan-Finch was to issue approximately 2,800,000 shares of new common stock. This stock was traded or used in the purchase of a publicly owned oil and gas corporation, a grain storage warehouse and several other properties and firms. In effect, Swan-Finch was becoming a sizable holding company, or so it appeared.

The master manipulator, however, had other plans for Swan-Finch. They were to consist of a series of dizzy stock-juggling acts that to this day confound the investigators who have attempted to reconstruct the financier's business activities. On January 10, 1956, Swan-Finch issued 527,427 new shares of common stock. These shares were supposed to be traded for 210,971 shares of Doeskin Products, the famous tissue manufacturer.

Control of Doeskin had fallen into Birrell's hands in 1947. The indefatigable financier acquired Doeskin by the simple expedient of selling the company two million dollars worth of securities, most of which were overvalued, and then using the proceeds to buy a controlling interest. Birrell's Doeskin shares were in turn held by Greater New York Industries, the former brewery that had become a Birrell-controlled holding company. For the next eight years Doeskin's stockholders could make few complaints. The financier had left the company in the hands of its experienced managers. From 1949 to 1955 annual sales had more than doubled, climbing to over nineteen million dollars. Profits after taxes came to over one-half million. Then in the annual report for 1955, the tissue maker announced the exchange of shares between Swan-Finch and Doeskin, appending this gratuitous note:

> This change in ownership of these shares does not affect the capital structure of Doeskin nor does it change the basic management policies of your company as Mr. Lowell M. Birrell who has been Chairman of Doeskin for the past seven years heads the active management of Swan-Finch Oil Corporation as President of that company.
>
> Swan-Finch Oil Corporation, which is over 100 years old, has been expanding and diversifying rapidly in the past few years and will place its facilities and resources at the disposal of Doeskin to aid in every way the development of our business.

The report so complimentary to Mr. Lowell M. Birrell was signed by Board Chairman Lowell M. Birrell. However, the statement that "Swan-Finch . . . will place its facilities and resources at the disposal of Doeskin to aid in every way the development of our business" was if anything misleading. The financier had no intention of truly developing the business of either Swan-Finch or Doeskin. He was interested, though, in developing the resources of a major stockholder, Birrell.

Here is what actually happened. The 500,000-odd shares of Swan-Finch that were supposed to reach Doeskin shareholders never did. Actually, they were turned over to Greater New York Industries and then funneled out to a series of

Birrell-controlled companies. In turn there is no record that Swan-Finch either received or benefited from the Doeskin shares. Instead, the shares of both Doeskin and Swan-Finch were dumped on the market in a series of complicated maneuvers, all designed to hide the stock's origin.

To illustrate the complexity of this cloaking operation let us trace the movement of a single certificate representing five thousand Swan-Finch common shares. These shares were given the Certificate Number CO 515. Here follows the true voyage of CO 515, from the docks of Swan-Finch, out into the securities channels of North America, finally emerging on the auction block of the American Stock Exchange. It was a saga unequaled in purposeful confusion.

The date of CO 515's launching was January 9, 1956, when Swan-Finch floated 125,000 shares. This new stock issue was part of the 500,000-odd shares that were supposed to be traded for the 200,000 shares of Doeskin. However, CO 515 was never to reach Doeskin's stockholders.

Not in the least surprising, one of the first things that happened to certificate CO 515 representing five thousand Swan-Finch shares was that it had its registry changed. Instead of sailing under the name of Lowell McAfee Birrell, its true owner, it was registered under the name of a New York broker. It next appeared in Greater New York Laboratories, a subsidiary of Greater New York Industries, the brewery that had become one of Birrell's holding companies. Then, in early February, 1956, a professional New York moneylender made a loan to Greater New York Laboratories Collateral for the loan included the peripatetic CO 515. The block of five thousand shares of Swan-Finch remained in the moneylender's custody until around mid-August when it was transferred to a nominee or dummy account of a bank in Montreal, Canada. CO 515 returned to the United States, arriving at a Canadian account of S & C Trading, purportedly a shell set up by Birrell which could be used as a stopping-off place for securities that he was juggling between one company and another. CO 515 was about to slip its mooring for the last time.

In early January, 1957, just one year after it had been launched by Swan-Finch, CO 515 arrived in the personal securities trading account of a race horse trainer named Charles A. Grande. CO 515 had come to Grande's account as part of a 30,000-share delivery against a payment of an $80,000 loan that had been made by the New York money-lender previously mentioned. It was then sold on the American Stock Exchange. CO 515 had never reached Doeskin's share owners for whom it was supposedly but not actually intended. CO 515, however, was not alone in its journeys. For hundreds of thousands of other shares of Swan-Finch stock were to take equally complicated routes before finally being sold to the public.

We can now begin to understand the complex task the S.E.C.'s investigators had in showing the origin of the Swan-Finch stock Birrell was dumping on the market. But the master manipulator had an even more important aim in mind than confounding the Federal agency's sleuths, and that was to sell large blocks of Swan-Finch without registering them with the Securities and Exchange Commission. By avoiding registration Birrell could sell Swan-Finch stock at highly inflated prices without informing the public as to the shares' true value. He managed to do this by drawing upon his extraordinary knowledge of the Securities laws and the Commission's rules.

The bona fide loan rule which Birrell employed worked

this way. An individual could borrow money from a money-lender, the borrower putting up securities as collateral for the loan. The moneylender would take the securities with the understanding that he would not sell them unless the borrower defaulted on his obligations. If the borrower did default because of financial adversity then the moneylender could sell the securities. Even though the sale of the securities might involve hundreds of thousands of dollars worth of shares, this would not be considered a public distribution. Neither the borrower nor the lender would have to register those shares with the S.E.C., thereby avoiding disclosure of the financial state of the company to the public.* Birrell used the moneylenders as one of his main funnels for dumping stock on the market and at the same time avoided the scrutiny that accompanies registration. Most important the financier, if necessary, could then claim in court that the swindle was perfectly legal.

Wall Street's moneylending industry, as Birrell himself knew, was and still is a bruising business that suffers neither fools nor amateurs. It is, I might add, the type of business which can prove highly profitable.

Not surprisingly, the Street's moneylenders really came into their own during the stock-market boom of the fifties. Investors and speculators frequently lacked the means to make the big-sized purchases of securities which would give them the large profits they sought. Some of the problems the speculators faced in increasing their purchasing power had been knowingly fostered by the Government. To keep the market from reacting like a runaway missile the Federal

* In *S.E.C. v. Guild Films Co., Inc.* (1960), the United States Court of Appeals for the Second Circuit upheld the Commission's contention that pledge transactions of the types described have no exemption from registration under the Securities Act.

Reserve Board raised margin requirements from 50 to 90 per cent.* What this meant was that anyone who bought $100 worth of stock had to put up $90 in cash. The restrictions became even harsher when the Government forbade banks or brokers to advance more than 10 per cent of the value of listed securities to anyone who planned to invest the cash in stocks. Thus, the type of speculation that easy credit creates had been strait-jacketed, or so the Federal Government thought. The Government, however, had not reckoned with the moneylenders, who, during the fifties at least, were not hemmed in by Federal credit margin requirements.

The moneylenders stepped into this tight credit gap with the speed of an emaciated boll weevil loosed in a cotton field. For almost any big-time speculator who had already accumulated $100,000 worth of securities, the moneylenders were willing to advance him as much as $90,000 in cash, which he could in turn use to buy more stocks. The interest rates which the speculator was asked to pay were astronomical, considering the huge sums he was borrowing. They usually averaged 2 per cent a month or 24 per cent a year. This meant that on a $90,000 loan extended over one year, the speculator paid out $21,600 in interest.

To put it another way, the high interest rate was the cover charge the securities gambler in the nineteen fifties had to pay to gain admission to the gaming tables. The chips he planned to play with were bought on the money he borrowed. And that was the point that separated the budding Baruchs from the stock market bumpkins. Most speculators, following the usual pattern, sought not only big but quick profits. This meant that they purchased highly volatile stock. If the stock shot upward everybody was happy. But if the

* At this writing it is 70 per cent.

price of the stock suddenly spun downward, the speculator could lose all he owned. It was not a game to be played by the weak in heart.

When Birrell first decided to approach the Street's moneylenders, the financier must have been well aware that he would be dealing with men as shrewd and tough as he. He must have known also that some men in the industry, made up of textile factors, real estate operators and professional lenders, were not always too particular about the source of the money they themselves borrowed to build up their own capital. These sources were not only varied but frequently were not the kind that would be forgiving if their own investments were dissipated. Though most lenders obtained their risk capital from friends and business associates, a few apparently were also willing to accept backing from the underworld or the so-called "smart money" that flows out of Las Vegas and Miami. Though Birrell deceived others, he must have realized he had to operate with considerable care in dealing with an industry some of whose members needed to account only to themselves and upon occasion the underworld elements they might have represented.

The scheme that Birrell was to use involving the moneylenders must have seemed at the time fool proof. He would put up about 400,000 shares of Swan-Finch and 200,000 shares of Doeskin as collateral to secure $1,500,000 in loans. The loans would be made to companies Birrell controlled. The financier would either fail to repay the loans or wait until the market value of the collateral stocks dropped. The moneylenders would then be able to claim the Swan-Finch and Doeskin stock were distress shares. In effect, they would be forced to sell the stock and without registering it with the S.E.C. Meanwhile, the $1,500,000 that had been loaned on the shares would disappear into the coffers of the Birrell-controlled companies.

The financier, of course, was not the type of man to leave anything to chance. The moneylenders were only a funnel through which the stock could be sold without registration. There yet remained the job of unloading the shares on the general public. A variety of means were to be used. They were to include the services of an extraordinary cast of characters. Among them were Charles A. Grande, the race-horse trainer previously mentioned; Gerard A. Re (known as Jerry Re), one of the top specialists on the floor of the American Exchange; his son, Gerard F. Re; Ernest Espinosa, a hanger-on and a partner in a well-known brokerage firm.

Though a major part of the distribution of the Swan-Finch stock began on December 18, 1956, the events themselves in a way had their beginning nearly a half-century before. It was then that Charles Grande and the elder Re first met, becoming boyhood friends in New York's Greenwich Village.

As each grew into manhood they sought out careers which though totally alien had one indefinable element in common, the necessary talent to make instinctive judgments. Grande's education ended upon graduation from P.S. No. 8. After a variety of jobs including working as a chauffeur and serving in the Army during World War I, he settled down to the occupation that was to bring him modest success. He became an expert trainer of race horses.

Meanwhile, Grande's boyhood friend, Jerry Re, decided to enter a business which in its way was as tricky and complicated as judging horseflesh. On December 8, 1920, the elder Re ventured into the securities market, becoming a member of what was later to be known as the American

Stock Exchange. As a securities' specialist he would trade directly on the Exchange's floor with representatives of other brokers. His primary function was to keep a fair and orderly market in the stocks assigned to him. To prevent erratic price movements in these securities he was supposed to buy when others sold and sell when others bought. The specialists job can be one of the most complex operations in the auction market. It entails not only a high degree of technical skill, but the equally imposing ability to judge the value of securities.

The elder Re, like his friend Grande, seemed eminently successful in the field he had chosen. Re, Re & Co., the firm the father helped organize, served as specialists for about twenty different securities. Despite their different interests, the friendship between Grande and the elder Re ripened with the horse trainer becoming the godfather of the stock expert's son. This friendship was also to prove profitable. One of the stocks for which Re, Re & Co. served as specialist was Swan-Finch. During the week of December 7, 1956, the elder Re was to receive a call from Lowell Birrell, telling him to come immediately to the financier's office. The elder Re later testified that Birrell told him with tears in his eyes that he was in serious financial difficulties and that the Swan-Finch stock that collateralized his loans would have to be sold. He asked the elder Re to help him.

In turn, Re sought out his friend Charles Grande. In July, 1954, about two and a half years prior to the major Swan-Finch distribution, an account had been opened in Grande's name at Josephthal & Co., a well-known brokerage house. Grande at the time had retired from training horses for "Red" Muckler and was facing some lean years. He was later asked by the S.E.C. why he opened an account at Josephthal.

GRANDE: To the best of my memory, how did I come to open that account? I was doing nothing. I was out of the horse business and being around with Jerry [Re] and his son and did I have—friends of his back and forth, talking here and there, I got a little interested and thought I wanted to go and gamble in the stock market.

QUESTION: Yes?

GRANDE: And previous to that I think he introduced me to Tony [Anthony Cordano, a partner in Josephthal] and I said something to Tony about opening an account down there at Josephthal's.

QUESTION: Who introduced you to Tony?

GRANDE: Jerry or his son Gerard or either one of them. It could have been both of them that were there when I met Tony.

The horse trainer, through whose brokerage account millions passed, played the classic role of the dummy or front. His ignorance of even the rudiments of the securities business was extraordinary, considering the large blocks of stocks traded in his name. Grande's lack of knowledge was brought out in an interrogation by the S.E.C.

QUESTION: Well, you sold 75 shares of the stock at 16⅞ and then you bought 75 shares at 16⅞, each for the same amount of money.

GRANDE: That's right.

QUESTION: Why did you do that?

GRANDE: I did a lot of them foolish things then.

QUESTION: What possible reason would you have to make that kind of a transaction?

GRANDE: I couldn't give you a reason for it now. I don't even know why I did it, but I did it and I was having a lot of fun.

In still further testimony, the S.E.C. probed Grande's understanding of the huge movement of securities through his account. Here is one more excerpt:

QUESTION: On January 7, 1955, you sold a large number of Thompson-Starrett shares. What was the occasion of that?

GRANDE: I sold a lot of them. I must have had them and I just kept selling them out. That's all. That was all.

QUESTION: You sold them all on one day?

GRANDE: Sold them on one day. It was one of them days I had a little wingding, I guess.

QUESTION: What do you mean by that?

GRANDE: Sitting in Semachio's apartment with what's his name, Josephthal—I guess Tony Cordano thought I was a crazy man or something.

Grande declared in a court affidavit, that around December 16, 1956, Jerry Re told him that he knew of certain large blocks of Swan-Finch Oil Corporation stock that had been pledged as collateral security for loans by Lowell Birrell "who was in financial difficulties." As a consequence, Grande's affidavit continued, these shares would be available for purchase as "distress shares" since there had been defaults on the loans and this collateral would have to be sold.

"I told Jerry Re," the horse trainer declared, "that I would be interested in the speculation; and at a social gathering he introduced me to one Ernest Espinosa who knew where the stock could be purchased. After I met Espinosa and he confirmed what Jerry Re had told me, I told Espinosa I would check my brokerage account and advise him the following day if I were in a position to take on the investment.

"The following day, in a telephone conversation, I told Espinosa I would buy the stock as soon as he notified me of its availability, and thereafter the stock deliveries to my account commenced and continued as set forth in the Becker affidavit.* Espinosa would inform me by telephone as additional lots of Swan-Finch stock became available through liquidation of collateral loans, and in each case I took the lots into my account with Josephthal [the horse trainer's broker]. As to the sales, I left no specific instructions with my brokers, but told them to use discretion and to get the best price they could."

Ernest Espinosa was typical of the dummy accounts and nominees used by Birrell in his manipulations. Espinosa later testified before the S.E.C. on how he met the financier and how Birrell in turn made use of him:

"I worked in New York with Mr. Poppleman in October of 1955, and I ran into Mr. Birrell at the Sherry Netherlands Hotel, and he invited me to his apartment for a drink, so when I got up there—that is when I first met Hector Rivero, a Cuban, and there were a lot of people there, maybe a dozen people and four or five Cubans, and I had a couple of drinks there, and he introduced me to all of these people, and said he was going down to the farm and he asked me to go down to the farm with him. So I said, sure. So he called up his wife, Mary, and said, 'I am going to put an old friend of yours on the phone,' and he put me on.

"I hadn't talked to her in a few years, and hadn't seen her, so I rode down to the farm with him, about nine o'clock we arrived. We took a Carey car down to the farm and that is when he told me that—he said, 'Ernie, we used to be real friendly years ago.' He said, 'In those days I had money, but I had no power, but I have power now.'

"I told him that I needed a job, that I was broke. So he told me, he said, 'Stick with me, you come with me, I'll make you rich.' So I stayed at the farm for about two weeks and he kept promising me these jobs and didn't give me one. Then he told me to get my clothes. So I went to Washington. I stayed three or

* Anthony Becker, one of the S.E.C.'s ablest senior investigators, spent nearly a year on the Swan-Finch case.

four days, got my clothes and returned to the farm. From then on, I hung around there, and he kept putting me off about getting me a job. And finally, one day, he came and told me, he said, 'We are going to Indiana tomorrow. I have a job for you. I am making you President of Continental Carnivar.' "

Not only did the account in Espinosa's name serve as a funnel for the Grande account but during an earlier four-month period (December 1955 to April 1956) the Res used the Espinosa dummy account at Josephthal to distribute Swan-Finch common stock valued at $315,510. Espinosa later testified that he never opened a brokerage account at Josephthal and that he had no knowledge of any of the transactions in the account in his name. During part of this period Espinosa received a salary of $125 a week. The salary was paid by Birrell.

Tony Becker, one of the crack S.E.C. investigators on the case, discovered that between December 18, 1956—two days after the elder Re approached his boyhood friend, Charles Grande—and March 12, some 470,000 Swan-Finch shares popped in and out of Grande's portfolio. This was approximately twenty per cent of all of Swan-Finch's outstanding common stock. Further, of the 470,000 shares that Grande was to have sold for him, about 388,000 shares were traded on the American Stock Exchange, where Re, Re & Co. were specialists in Swan-Finch.

According to an S.E.C. brief, the Res would use the dummy accounts as the means of controlling the distribution via the Exchange. Cordano, the brokerage partner who serviced the dummy accounts at Josephthal, was instructed to give all the orders in these accounts to the Res for execution with respect to the time and prices at which the shares were to be purchased or sold. On the floor of the Exchange, the Josephthal floor partner would then hand the orders to the Res and disclose to them the name of the particular dummy account for which the order was being executed. These orders would be executed by the elder or junior Re, both Stock Exchange specialists, at a price and at a time that would not break the market price.

Every effort was made through the entire distribution to show that all parties were abiding by the S.E.C.'s regulations. One of the most important rules aimed at protecting the public is that the sale of all control shares* must be registered with the Commission. Particular pains were taken by all those concerned with the Swan-Finch sales to inquire as to whether the shares involved came from "control" sources. The younger Re was to testify later that each time he was asked by the people at Josephthal and Grande as to whether the stock came from control sources, he called Birrell who assured him that they were not control shares.

Anthony Cordano, the partner in Josephthal who handled the horse trainer's account, told S.E.C. investigator Becker, "Each and every time that Mr. Grande instructed us to receive any shares of Swan-Finch, before the actual shares were received and paid for, I personally spoke with Mr. Grande and asked him the question 'Are these shares control shares?' " In each case, Cordano declared, Grande replied in the negative.

Cordano further testified that when the various deliveries were made not a single share of stock was registered in the name of the management of Swan-Finch and that the great bulk of certificates were in Street names.

Grande himself was to testify in his affidavit that he

---

* Control shares mean that the owner of such shares can influence the policy of the company the securities represent.

neither knew nor had any contact with Birrell or anyone in the management or control of Swan-Finch. He declared, "In the case of each delivery of Swan-Finch stock to my account, I gave defendant Cordano a letter of instructions advising Josephthal to receive it for my account. At the time I furnished the letters Mr. Cordano asked me whether I knew the actual source of these shares, and [I] informed him that on the basis of information furnished to me as hereinafter set forth, they were 'distress shares' being liquidated as loan collateral. In my first instruction letters Cordano suggested the addition on the reverse side of the phrase: 'The stock in question is not being sold for anyone who stands in a control relationship within the meaning of the Securities and Exchange Commission Act of 1933.' As is set forth in the Becker affidavit, although somewhat unclear in the form stated, this language was not supplied by me but Mr. Cordano and added at Cordano's request. The insertion of this phrase in the letters was explained to me by Cordano as a necessary formality for receiving the stock for transfer, and some of the letters were prepared in the Josephthal offices on typewriters there."

All these claims added up to one rather startling fact. By insisting that the Swan-Finch stock were not control shares, the participants in the sale could claim there had been no need to register the securities with the Commission. Thus there was no violation of the S.E.C. regulations. Not only were the participants protecting themselves from Commission charges but they also had provided a legal alibi for Birrell. In effect the master manipulator ended up with the seemingly perfect defense. No one including himself had in any way violated any laws. It would appear that the dumping of Swan-Finch stock was the financier's masterpiece.

Though no exact figures are known, the Swan-Finch manipulations were undoubtedly highly profitable to those chiefly connected with it. Cordano testified that because Grande's account had been introduced to his firm by the elder Re, the common Street practice was followed whereby Re, Re & Co. and Josephthal split the commissions on all of the Grande Swan-Finch shares sold on the American Stock Exchange.* Grande himself insisted that he made little if any profit despite the fact that at least $2,870,000 in unregistered securities (including others besides Swan-Finch) were distributed through Grande's account to the public over a three-year period. The itinerant horse trainer whose ignorance of the stock market was admittedly monumental was questioned later by the S.E.C. on whether he had made a profit:

QUESTION: Did you make money or lose money in the stock market?

GRANDE: I didn't make any.

QUESTION: You never made any net?

GRANDE: I may have made a few when it winds up, when I got out of it. I don't think—maybe I made my living expenses out of it.

QUESTION: That is all?

GRANDE: That's all. That's why I went back in the horse business. I took some of that money and I went back in the horse business with it.

* The Res have been accused by Government investigators of the most flagrant series of market manipulations in the more than twenty-five-year history of the Securities Act. In fact, Swan-Finch was only one facet of their operation, which will be discussed in more detail in Chapter 7. (On October 15, 1961, the American Stock Exchange expelled Anthony Cordano, an allied member of the exchange, and levied maximum fines of $5,000 each against two other partners of Josephthal. On the same day the New York Stock Exchange said Cordano's allied membership on the Big Board had automatically terminated.)

QUESTION: How much money did you go back in the horse business with?

GRANDE: I put about—gee, I put close to nine—I put about $13,000 back in the horse business.

However, for Birrell and the companies he controlled the profits must have been huge indeed. Through a variety of tributaries including a Canadian garage mechanic whom he had met in a New York night club, Birrell's dominated firms eventually distributed 1,200,000 shares of Swan-Finch and 400,000 shares of Doeskin. The average selling price for Swan-Finch was $4 a share; for Doeskin, $8. Thus, the price the public paid for Swan-Finch and Doeskin stock totaled around eight million dollars.

It was at about this point that Windels received the angry millionaire's phone call concerning Birrell's operations. The information the informant passed on, however, did not come as a complete surprise to the government official. Even before the millionaire unburdened himself, the head of the S.E.C.'s New York office had already begun an informal investigation of Birrell. During the early Tellier probe and his visit to the windswept Colorado Plateau the previous year, Windels had been told by a mining promoter, "The law will never catch up with Lowell M. Birrell." During the ensuing months Birrell's name kept cropping up and Windels ordered the market surveillance department to collect as much confidential information as possible on the financier's operations and empire. But the Regional Administrator's orders included a command that the investigation would have to be made with utmost discretion, for Windels had no desire to show the S.E.C.'s hand until he was ready to press for a full probe. That opportunity came in early February, 1957.

Windels' informant had indicated that Swan-Finch, which Birrell controlled, was being unloaded on the American Stock Exchange. The S.E.C. Administrator also had been informed that the financier had been looting Swan-Finch of its assets.

"Even though Birrell was in effect embezzling Swan-Finch," Windels recalled, "we could not get him on a charge of failing to file a report exposing what he was doing to the company. Although the stock was traded on the American Exchange, the fact that it was in the unlisted category meant that Birrell did not have to file the usual reports. Furthermore, while the assets were being removed from Swan-Finch, the stock was increasing in price. I knew that Birrell had to be unloading against a manipulated market. That's when I ordered a full probe."

The S.E.C.'s investigation, however, unearthed another series of problems that at first glance seemed to make prosecution impossible. "It appeared," Windels said, "that Swan-Finch was being sold by moneylending groups which obtained the shares as the result of defaulted loans. The moneylenders, in turn, claimed that registration was not necessary because of the 'bonafide loan exemptions.' They and Birrell seemed to have an excellent defense. It looked pretty grim. Then we hit upon the idea of making a frontal attack. Our case would be the simple truth, that the so-called sale of 'distressed shares' was just a subterfuge to sell stock without registering it. In effect, Birrell was hiding behind the bonafide loan exemption. Furthermore, we would claim that the moneylenders were actually serving as underwriters and that the two per cent monthly interest charge on the loans to Birrell was their commission for selling the stock.

But the going promised to be rough. There was simply no legal precedent."

The case was assigned to Jack Devaney and Eileen Evers, a pert blonde and a top enforcement attorney. Miss Evers presented the Commission's charge before Federal Judge Sidney Sugarman and on April 15, 1957, obtained a temporary restraining order to halt the sale of Swan-Finch stock unless registered with the S.E.C. Among the twenty-four defendants involved in the order were Birrell, the Res, Josephthal, Grande and the moneylenders. On the following day the American Stock Exchange suspended trading in Swan-Finch. Then, seven days later, one of the moneylenders submitted a surprise motion to lift the restraining order as it affected his firm. Judge Sugarman agreed and the order was vacated.

"When Jack Devaney told me what had happened," Windels recalled, "I was really taken aback. Here we had Birrell in court and for the first time in twenty years it looked as if the Government could do something. Now the whole case was hanging by an eyelash."

Judge Sugarman's dismissal order came late in the afternoon. The next morning Windels appealed the order to Judge Harold Medina of the Circuit Court of Appeals. Meanwhile, the S.E.C. investigators closely followed that days's trading. As a result Windels was able to inform Judge Medina that the remaining Birrell-originated Swan-Finch stock was being dumped on the market. Less than forty-eight hours after the order had been vacated it was reinstated by Judge Medina. Then on June 27, as the case was called for trial nearly all the defendants, including Birrell, consented to a permanent injunction. One of those, however, who did not was a moneylender.

For Windels and the S.E.C., it was the opportunity they had hoped for. During the scheduled trial involving the moneylender, the Commission would be able to call Birrell and have him testify under oath concerning his activities with Swan-Finch. At last the financier's activities would be exposed to public scrutiny. Windels knew the testimony would prove devastating.

And so, apparently, did Birrell. Repeated attempts by the Commission to serve the financier with a subpoena and thus place him on the witness stand always met the same frustrating end. Birrell could not be found. Then, in early May, S.E.C. investigators learned that Echo Falls Farm would be the site of a gala benefit horse show for Eagle Volunteer Fire Company No. 1. Not only would the horsy set from Maryland and Virginia be there, but so would three thousand other people. Windels calculated that it would be the type of show that would appeal to Birrell's ego and that the financier would undoubtedly make his appearance.

The subpoena serving assignment was given to senior S.E.C. Investigator Bruce Hilsee. Hilsee, who had been with the Commission for eighteen years, had followed the Birrell case with more than passing interest. He also happened to live only a short drive from Birrell's estate.

"I didn't want to appear conspicuous," Hilsee recalled, "so I dressed in what I thought were horse clothes, a sports shirt and contrasting slacks. Then I drove over to Echo Falls and parked my car in the south pasture. The place was jammed. For the next hour I wandered around looking for Birrell. But I couldn't find him. Then my eye fell on a state trooper. He had been assigned to guide traffic. I asked him if he knew Birrell. 'Sure,' he replied, 'and I'll introduce you to him.' We walked a little way and then he nodded toward a man in a blue sports jacket decorated with a coat of arms. I handed him the subpoena. He took one glance at it and just shrugged. He didn't seem angry. It was as though he was expecting it."

That was in May. During that summer a series of reports had placed Birrell in nearly a half-dozen countries including France, Guatemala and Venezuela. The moneylender's trial was scheduled for the fall. To keep the pressure on the financier and to insure his attendance, Windels decided to have a second subpoena served. Again Hilsee was given the assignment. This time a tip filtered into the S.E.C. network that Birrell was in Canada and that he planned to fly to Cuba. The plane would make a stop at Idlewild, New York. As Birrell stepped onto the landing field, Hilsee thrust the second subpoena into his hand. The man who could never forget a face took one look at the investigator and murmured, "You again."

Those two words were Birrell's last utterance on American soil. After an extended stay in Cuba and Europe, he flew to Brazil, the one country which at the time could offer him protection from the ubiquitous Bruce Hilsee and the long arm of the Securities and Exchange Commission. For Brazil was then the only country in the Western Hemisphere that did not have an extradition treaty with the United States. Birrell, so it seemed, had swindled thousands of innocent stockholders, bled numerous corporations, and had got away with it.

It is unlikely that his day of judgment will ever come. On January 13, 1961, a little more than three years after the financier fled the United States, this country and Brazil signed an extradition treaty.* But the agreement, according to the Brazilian Justice Ministry, does not provide for the extradition of people wanted for crimes before the treaty came into force. Presently the United States is awaiting for Brazil to vote ratification.

Birrell, however, has two additional safeguards. First, the Brazilian government has charged him with entering the country illegally—he came in on a Canadian passport. As long as there is a charge against him in the Brazilian courts, he cannot be extradited. Second, he could avoid extradition by becoming the father of a child born in Brazil. It remains to be seen whether Birrell will take advantage of still one more loophole in the law.

If Birrell should somehow be forced to return to these shores—he insists that he is waiting until the time is propitious—the financier will find himself facing an impressive array of charges. He will be kept busy battling a sixty-nine-count grand larceny indictment handed down by the New York Grand Jury in July, 1959. The Grand Jury contends that Birrell was responsible for swindling stockholders out of fourteen million dollars in the manipulation of Swan-Finch and Doeskin stock.† He will also face a suit brought by the trustees of Swan-Finch, which was put into receivership. In the Swan-Finch suit he is charged with causing losses of eight and one-half million dollars. He has also been indicted on embezzling charges and the U. S. Internal Revenue Depart-

* Brazil, which has no capital punishment, had refused to sign an extradition treaty with the United States, which does permit the death penalty. Under the treaty Brazil reserves the right to withhold extradition unless it is convinced the fugitive would not be executed.

† Actually Birrell faces two indictments involving his operations in connection with Doeskin Products. The second one was handed down by a Federal Grand Jury on March 1, 1961.

ment has charged Birrell with evading nearly four million dollars in income taxes.

Meanwhile, Lowell McAfee Birrell, a man who possessed one of the most brilliant financial minds of this century, squanders his remaining days in Rio de Janeiro. Still the man of mystery, no one truly knows how he spends his time. Some who have seen him insist that he is drinking more than ever before. And an American physician who resides in Rio says the financier talked him into investing $250,000 in an electrical hardware factory in the Matto Grosso. The physician contends that after he handed over the money Birrell disappeared. The electrical hardware factory? According to the physician it never existed.

5. THE GIN RUMMY EXPERT FROM SIBERIA

At the height of his career Alexander Leonard "Kid Sandy McSande" Guterma was asked to explain the phenomenal success of his financial ventures. "They are run," he declared, "by a goddamn genius."

And in a way he was right. By the age of forty-one Alexander Guterma simultaneously headed three multimillion dollar corporations listed on the New York Stock Exchange, a feat so far unequalled by anyone. What made this achievement appear so remarkable was that within six years he had risen from almost total anonymity to rule a major auto-parts manufacturer, a large Hollywood and TV studio, a national radio network, one of the nation's oldest makers of household cleaning compounds, a brokerage firm, not to mention such secondary ventures as cattle, oil and uranium. What no one knew at the time was that this corporate genius also happened to be one of the cleverest financial pirates who ever operated on Wall Street.

Though this owlish-looking man with the unassuming features of a suit salesman did not become a Wall Street legend until the middle 1950's, his earlier career proved equally fantastic. By Guterma's own claim he was born in Irkutsk in eastern Siberia on April 29, 1915, the son of a "Protestant General" in the Czar's Army. With the outbreak of the Russian Revolution, Guterma's parents, who have been variously described as Russian, Polish, Estonian and Czech, took their infant son to China where the boy's father is supposed to have wandered up and down the coast selling jewelry. Besides living in such cities as Tientsin, Shanghai and Harbin, he apparently resided long enough in Tsingtao, China, to graduate from a missionary school.

One story, perhaps apocryphal but in character, was that Guterma took up boxing while studying at the missionary school. He became so proficient that he was crowned the lightweight champion of Shanghai at eighteen. It wasn't long before the future financier was billed as Kid Sandy McSande after an old and popular China-coast fighter.

The events of the next fifteen years are shrouded in that intriguing mystery so typical of the man himself. According to the Guterma version he became friendly with a detachment of Marines stationed on the China coast. An adventurous lad, he decided to join his friends who were returning to the United States. Dressing in olive drabs, he stowed away on one of the transport ships. As soon as the boat reached Honolulu Guterma went ashore and soon obtained a job in a radio repair shop. But soon the U.S. immigration authorities were questioning him. Guterma denied that he had any knowledge of such things as the immigration laws and had declared in his work permit that he was born in Brooklyn and therefore was to be considered an American citizen. A routine checkup, however, disclosed that Guterma originally came from Siberia, not Flatbush, a distinction of some significance according to the United States immigration service. It wasn't long before Alexander Guterma was on the high seas again bound for China.

The Guterma version of his peregrinations is simple enough. He was a young man with an adventurous turn of mind who went to Honolulu because, said Guterma, "I figured there was opportunity here [in Hawaii] better than I could get in China."

This version has been denied by Jerome G. Londin, then an executive assistant United States attorney, who years later prosecuted the Government's major case against the financier. Londin declared in court that shortly before Guterma left for Hawaii he found himself in trouble with the law. According to the Government prosecutor Guterma's criminal record goes back to 1935, when he was twenty.

"It arose during his time in Tientsin, China," Londin continued. "He [Guterma] misappropriated funds there, according to the Government's information, and he fled to Shanghai, which indicates that he is a man who is not amenable to the processes of the law. In Shanghai he was apprehended and brought back to Tientsin, and, according to the Government's information, on February 5, 1935, he received a sentence of six months imprisonment for this offense. After his release he stowed away to Hawaii."

Years later, when Guterma's operations were being exposed in front-page headlines, a spokesman for the financier held a press conference and told the assembled reporters that when he discovered he was in Hawaii illegally, Sandy Guterma "voluntarily returned to the Far East."

"Not so," declared Government Attorney Jerome Londin

who told a Federal court that young Guterma once again stowed away. This time it was on a China-bound boat without the knowledge of the authorities and while under deportation orders.

"Why did he depart so precipitously?" Londin asked rhetorically. "Why didn't he wait and let his expenses be paid by the Government? They were going to deport him. He didn't have to stow away on a ship.

"Well," added Londin, "he had a little trouble there [Hawaii] according to the Government's information. He had worked for a radio corporation, and in connection with his employment subsequent to the warrant of deportation dated December 4, 1935, and before he stowed away on January 11, 1936, we find the motive for his stowing away and not waiting to go out at Government expense.

"There were lodged against him five separate charges, three of embezzlement and two of forgery. They were very minor items, $50, $100, $125. The details need not concern this Court. But that is the reason, the Government submits, for his stowing away and going off back to China, not because he suddenly learned about laws and that he was in Hawaii illegally, and that he decided that he would be a law-abiding citizen and leave of his own accord."

During the next decade Guterma like millions of others was caught up in the war that enveloped the world. However, where others found themselves helplessly driven by the ensuing chaos, Sandy Guterma managed to outwit events and prosper.

According to one story, which the financier has stoutly denied, Guterma returned to the Orient and fell in with a group of pirates that operated off the China coast. He is supposed to have given them financial backing. He is also supposed to have operated a fishing fleet that sailed out of Shanghai under a Czechoslovakian flag.

Sometime in the late 1930's Guterma arrived in the Philippines. According to U. S. Attorney Londin he made the trip under a false Czechoslovakian passport which he had purchased. Then, on April 30, 1941, Guterma married Anita McGrath, the daughter of an American citizen and shoe manufacturer. Seven months later the Japanese bombed Pearl Harbor.

Shortly after the Japanese invasion of the Philippines Guterma was summarily placed in a concentration camp. The invaders thought he was an American. He was released when he proved to Japanese satisfaction that he came from Siberia, an event tinged with some irony considering that Guterma spent the remaining portion of his life acquiring American habits, mannerisms and money.

No sooner was he freed—he only spent a few weeks in Japanese hands—than this son of a Russian general applied his wits to making ends meet. And meet they did in the form of a successful gambling casino, a general store known as Escolia Auction and Exchange, and some sharp trading in the money market. How Guterma got started in all these ventures still remains a mystery. What is known is that by the end of the war Alexander Guterma emerged as a moderately prosperous wheeler and dealer. As the result of his wartime business operations he found himself on the "blocked list" of both the United States and Philippine treasuries. This meant he had to obtain special licenses for future ventures. As Guterma later summed it up: "What else could I do? I had to live."

Those early post-war years finally offered Guterma the

chance he had so long been seeking. He began by playing the securities market in the Philippines and was so busy trading that a number of acquaintances thought he was a broker. Somewhere along the way he met and impressed one of Manila's sugar kings, J. Amanda Araneta. Araneta's holdings had largely been destroyed as the result of the war. Guterma was hired to help put things right. One of his jobs included rebuilding a sugar mill. He was promoted to a junior executive position and in short order came up with a plan that was to net him a small fortune.

Raw sugar, Guterma discovered, is usually packed in gunny sacks made out of jute. He also learned that most of the world's raw jute was grown in the steamy Bengal jungles that divide Pakistan and India. Guterma took advantage of this information after World War II when the Kashmir curtain cut off Pakistan's export of jute to neighboring India.

So, the story goes, the budding financier arrived in Pakistan where he persuaded officials there to sell their country's jute crop to Araneta. His next stop was Italy where he leased several large textile factories that began manufacturing gunny sacks out of Pakistani jute. His Philippine employer generously gave him an estimated $500,000 as his share of the profits. Guterma was ready to enter the promised land of milk and money.

His arrival in Los Angeles in 1950 went unnoticed, not surprising since few people knew him. Among those who did, probably no one suspected that within six years he would rule a twenty-five-million-dollar empire. Even his very appearance seemed to hide his talents. Virtually bald, with a prominent, fleshy nose that juts out between large-lensed glasses, a wide mouth, and breast pocket invariably stuffed with Corona Coronas, Sandy Guterma did not look like a man who could command other men's futures. How he managed can be explained in part by his extraordinary charm. A tongue laden with gab, he seemed never to run out of anecdotes and humorous stories which he told with gusto. An able linguist, he could fill a conversation with descriptive expressions in Russian, Spanish, German, English, Chinese and Tagalog which he learned in the Philippines. Buoyant, outgoing—"Everybody calls me Sandy," would be his greeting—Alexander Guterma had that special quality of the successful. He could always sell himself. There were, as we shall see, an extraordinary list of buyers.

Guterma's initial commercial effort was typical of his ability to turn a quick profit. Arriving in California he bought a home and then a few days later decided to move to New York. His profit on the sale of the house came to $8,000. He was on his way.

No sooner did Guterma reach New York than he departed, this time to Palm Beach, Florida. The man from Irkutsk learned that Japan's source of ramie, a cotton-like fiber, had been cut off by the Chinese Communists, which opened the field to Sandy Guterma. He had also been told that kenaf, another fiber, would make an excellent substitute for jute. Florida sun and soil were ideal for the growth of both. With a three-quarter-of-a-million-dollar bankroll gathered from Filipino investors plus $140,000 of his own money, Guterma planted nearly one thousand acres. The profit apparently wasn't too large and Guterma and his backers parted, the financier receiving the land under cultivation. What later proved ideal about the arrangement was that the one thousand acres of Florida soil were to become the springboard for Guterma's multimillion-dollar empire.

Guterma's first step was to organize Shawano Development Corporation, whose chief asset at the time consisted of 920 acres, fully irrigated, plus an additional 10,240 acres of Florida real estate that still needed some water control work. In the process he merged into Shawano the separate kenaf and ramie companies which he purchased from his Filipino backers for $75,000. While these matters were being taken care of, Guterma, exuding charm, enlisted the backing of several highly placed and well-respected citizens, including Charley E. Johns, former governor of Florida, John K. Colgate, a Colgate-Palmolive director and representatives of Foremost Dairy interests, all of whom became directors of Shawano Development Corporation. Meanwhile, Shawano issued over 100,000 shares, made proper notification to the S.E.C. and then began selling its stock to the public. One of the brokerage houses that handled this underwriting was McGrath Securities Corporation, which Guterma had founded in 1953, and apparently named after his wife, the former Anita McGrath. Only a few years later the S.E.C. was to describe McGrath Securities as a boiler-room operation from its inception.

An example of the brokerage firm's selling techniques was a three-foot-long brochure touting the virtues of Shawano and its chief product, the ineffable ramie. The brochure included seven snapshots of the Shawano plantations as well as a sketchy map of central Florida showing the Development Corporation's approximate location. Its eloquence, however, was devoted to ramie. After noting that Shawano's entire 1954 crop had been sold to a Japanese business concern, the brochure described ramie's numerous uses: "The ancient Egyptians used it to wrap mummies, and ramie was cited in a Chinese report on agriculture about 4,000 years ago. The superior mildew resistance of Japanese uniforms in the last war was traced to the use of ramie." It concluded by forecasting that "ramie seems assured of a successful future in the textile market" through the wise use of blends with other fabrics. Needless to say, Shawano's first stock issue did exceedingly well with the public buying more than 100,000 shares. For Guterma, the rewards of the securities market had become self-evident.

During the ensuing months Shawano, under Guterma's guidance, was to issue approximately eighteen million shares. These shares, in turn, were exchanged for a Florida dairy herd, a resort hotel in Miami, mercury mining claims in Oregon and Nevada, Wyoming uranium deposits, and sixty-three oil wells in Wyoming and Kansas. Then began an effective campaign of hyperbole including several unduly optimistic reports that appeared in the financial column of a New York newspaper and a market advisory service. These fillips were all that the boiler-room salesmen needed and it wasn't long before some fifteen thousand investors had paid out over ten million dollars for Shawano securities. Within three years Shawano Development Corporation was to sink quietly into bankruptcy. Guterma, though, had already left the helm and was safely ensconced on dry land.*

It appears that while the financial world was drawing few lessons from the financier's operations, Guterma was to become even more daring. He was willing to take chances that others would shun out of honesty or fear. Like Birrell he apparently made a careful study of the S.E.C. regulations, and then, when it suited his own ends, ignored them. But most important, he seems to have thrived on the risks in-

---

* As the result of information turned up by the S.E.C.'s Eddy Jaegerman, a Federal indictment was handed down in September, 1961, charging the fraudulent sale of Shawano stock. Guterma was named a co-conspirator, but not a defendant.

volved. Typical of Guterma's love of gambling was his penchant for gin rummy. He would play while waiting for phone calls from his associates in Europe, Canada or the West Coast, winning or losing thousands on the turn of a card. But the financier's main wager was the play around the corporate table.

For Guterma the time of the big plunge was 1955 and 1956. In those two years he acquired control of United Dye and Chemical, Bon Ami, a manufacturer of household cleaning compounds, and F. L. Jacobs, an auto-parts manufacturer. All three were listed on the New York Stock Exchange, a fact that understandably seemed to impress the investing public with the financier's business acumen. Eventually this impression of financial legerdemain was to prove costly for the thousands who preferred to believe that Guterma's Midas touch would rub off on them.

Guterma's first large acquisition consisted of a controlling interest in United Dye and Chemical, which, with the aid of some of his former Shawano associates, he purchased for about $400,000 dollars. The stock had been previously owned by Lowell Birrell, the master manipulator described earlier. Birrell had looted the company of some two million dollars' worth of assets, a fact that was generally unknown to the public at the time. Utilizing the same techniques that were employed in the dumping of Shawano, United Dye shares quadrupled in price in less than six months, then plummeted. Guterma, meanwhile, had secretly sold out his own shares at a handsome profit. It wasn't until February, 1958, that the New York Stock Exchange delisted United Dye. That was two and a half years after Guterma had netted a profit of about one million dollars.

The financier's second conquest was the long-established

household cleansing manufacturer, the Bon Ami Company, whose controlling shares United Dye purchased for over two million dollars in cash on May 2, 1956. At the annual stockholders' meeting a year later a number of Guterma's associates were elected to Bon Ami's board of directors, including Robert J. Eveleigh, Guterma's trusted aide, who had served as a director of United Dye. Guterma himself was named Bon Ami board chairman. According to a Bon Ami stockholders' suit filed in April, 1958, the financier and his associates managed in a variety of ways to dissipate over two million dollars worth of the corporation's assets within a year and a half.

Typical of Guterma's trickery, according to the suit, was an arrangement that allowed the financier to unload the 90,000 Bon Ami shares United Dye had originally purchased which gave Guterma control of the cleansing manufacturer. As the result of dumping the 90,000 shares, the suit contended, Bon Ami was bilked out of $900,000. Involved in the deal was a promoter with the improbable name of Sortiris Galahad Fassoulis, who began international trading operations with $5,000 in capital at the end of World War II. By the time Fassoulis met Guterma, the former had lost at least one fortune and was in need of a helping hand.

On August 19, 1957, the stockholders claimed, Fassoulis, under Guterma's guidance, founded Baltic Investment Corporation. On the very next day Baltic purchased from United Dye and Chemical the 90,000 shares of Bon Ami stock. On the surface at least this meant that Baltic and not United Dye controlled Bon Ami. The price Baltic paid United Dye for the Bon Ami stock came to $1,700,000. This was $500,000 more than the market value and thus an immediate half-million-dollar paper profit for United Dye. Nine hundred thousand dollars, or about one-half the money paid by Baltic to United Dye came from various moneylenders. Fittingly, the Bon Ami shares that Baltic purchased were used as security for the loans. So far Fassoulis, under Guterma's guidance, had raised only half the purchase price of the Bon Ami shares. Further, Bon Ami was in no way directly involved. The next step was to cause Bon Ami itself to lose nearly one million dollars.

One of Fassoulis' numerous projects included the control of a Panamanian company known as Icthyan Associates, S.A., which owned the television rights to 170 films, most of them foreign. These rights were worth approximately $150,-000, the price Fassoulis had paid for them. Under the rights agreement Europe was about the only place the films could be shown. These rights in turn were sold by Fassoulis and Icthyan to Bon Ami for the inflated sum of over one million dollars. The money was then handed to United Dye. If one follows these deals carefully, one will note the final irony—Fassoulis, a total stranger to Bon Ami, had purchased Bon Ami stock with Bon Ami's own money. No one seems to know whether Guterma personally benefited from this corporate finesse. The financier contends that he had already given up control of United Dye which had owned and then sold the 90,000 Bon Ami shares. However, the stockholders in their suit contended that Guterma was directly involved with Fassoulis' alleged machinations.

One thing, though, is certain at this point. Within six short years since his arrival in the United States Alexander Guterma was living in the affluent style of a Kuwait sheik. He resided in an eighty-thousand-dollar English Tudor house in Fairfield County, Connecticut. He traveled around in a Dual Ghia sports car, two Cadillacs and a ninety-foot yacht and claimed membership in the Huntington, Manila and Guam yacht clubs. As the result of his business connections he had at his disposal a $375,000 pine-paneled Convair airplane. A generous man, he lavished on his wife expensive diamond, emerald and pearl necklaces, earrings and pins. (Later, when he achieved unwelcome notoriety in the newspapers two thieves entered his New York hotel suite and announced to his wife and fourteen-year-old daughter who were alone: "We've come for the jewelry," then managed to collect $60,000 worth of precious gems.)

His working habitat was equally expansive. His own office was covered with wall-to-wall gold-thread carpeting. For decoration, he hung the walls with rare Philippine paintings and filled large teakwood cabinets with exquisite jade carvings.

During his idle hours Guterma would sail in his yacht along the Florida coast or visit New York's more expensive night clubs. A connoisseur of the ordinary, he displayed an encyclopedic knowledge of American sports that astounded the natives. He also showed an intimate knowledge of the city's East Side delicatessens, ordering special meats and cheeses in a pronounced Brooklyn accent. The high point in the financier's Americanization came on November 9, 1956, when the immigrant from Irkutsk was granted United States citizenship. It appeared at the time that Alexander Leonard Guterma had fulfilled his aspirations. But the financier had larger dreams. Several months before he became an American citizen, Guterma began laying the foundation for a financial empire that would eventually stretch from New York to California and from Michigan to Texas.

Guterma's boldest venture got under way in the spring and summer of 1956, when he made his first purchase of the

stock of F. L. Jacobs. Jacobs, a Michigan auto-parts manufacturer, was an old, established company that had been in
business for over forty years. For those four decades it had
remained under the managership of the relatives of its
founder. In large measure its prosperity was tied to the
fortunes of Detroit and the auto industry. The firm's success
also rested on the ability of inherited leadership. And as
sometimes happens in family-run concerns this leadership
was found wanting. Sometime after World War II an insurgent Stockholders' Protective Committee was formed.
Though unknown to the participants and Guterma himself, the battle over control of the auto-parts manufacturer
was indirectly to open the corporation's treasury to the financier.

One member of the Stockholders' Protective Committee
was a man by the name of Frank E. Howard. Howard's
background is of some interest in that he is fairly typical of
the men who enlist in the proxy wars that have of late
rumbled through so many corporations. Howard began his
career in the early 1930's by writing specially assigned articles on business and economics for various newspapers. He
moved into public relations and investment counseling when
he attracted the attention of Lowell Birrell while giving a
talk before a Stock Exchange group. Apparently as a result
of the impression that he made, Howard became public
relations representative for two Birrell-controlled companies,
Greater New York Industries and Doeskin Products Corporation. Howard contends, however, that he never served as
the financier's personal public relations representative and
that the Birrell-controlled companies were only a few of
his clients which also included Twentieth Century Fox,
RKO Theatres and the Hudson & Manhattan Railroad.

It wasn't too long before the public relations expert and former financial writer employed his talents in a number of proxy fights. Though he was usually retained by management he also joined several opposition groups. One of them included the insurgent committee at F. L. Jacobs. In part as a result of Howard's guidance, the Stockholders' Protective Committee were able to oust management. Howard in turn was elected a director and then in October, 1953, became Chairman of the Board.

Though Howard and his associates managed to put Jacobs in the black—it had been operating at a deficit—the auto-parts manufacturer again went into the red. It was apparently at this point that Howard and others decided to sell out. The purchaser was Alexander Guterma who gave Howard and his family $250,000 for more than 27,000 shares of Jacobs' stock. The sale was made on March 1, 1956. Two months later Guterma was elected Chairman of the Board and President of F. L. Jacobs, positions he was to hold for the next three years. In effect, through the purchase of less than three per cent of the company's outstanding stock, the financier had gained control and had become the principal officer of a corporation whose assets were soon to be worth over twenty million dollars. Eventually, Guterma's stock holdings in Jacobs were to reach nearly 150,000 shares at a value of about one million dollars.

At the time that Guterma first took over Jacobs, the company's operations were limited to serving the auto industry. It was a business its former executives knew well and could handle. Under the financier's direction, however, Jacobs began to expand at a swift rate, gaining control of such diverse operations as Scranton Corporation, a manufacturer of lace, window curtains and place mats, with plants in Pennsylvania and Illinois; Hal Roach Studios, with movie and TV production facilities in Culver City, California; and Mutual Broadcasting System, a radio network that covered the entire nation. These acquisitions were made through various exchanges of stock with Scranton becoming a subsidiary of Jacobs and Hal Roach Studios becoming a subsidiary of Scranton. During Guterma's stewardship Jacobs also controlled Storm-Vulcan, which made airplane parts in Texas, and Symphonic Electronics, which made phonograph and stereo equipment. By February 28, 1958, the structure of F. L. Jacobs had changed to the point where it was no longer considered a manufacturing concern but a holding company whose subsidiaries took care of their own day-to-day operations. It was in truth a highly complex corporate maze with an equally complex set of books. Under the circumstances it would appear understandable that a certain number of items such as assets, securities and cash could somehow flow from one subsidiary to the next and then dribble away without any of Jacobs' 2,500 ordinary stockholders being the wiser. For the financier the situation was opportune for some fancy finagling. According to the Government this sleight-of-hand maneuvering was to cost Jacobs over one million dollars in just one operation alone.

The key to all of this as well as much of Guterma's shadowy dealing involving Jacobs was a company by the name of Comficor. Comficor was nothing more than a combination funnel and siphon for the financier's operations. For obvious reasons, Guterma insisted for a long period of time that he did not control Comficor, an innocuous holding company that bought stock and borrowed money. Just how Guterma managed to keep secret his connections with Comficor was told in detail by Salvatore R. Pavis, at the financier's trial. Pavis was the manager of the burlap department of Bunge Corporation, a world-wide trader in bulk commodities. He was also a friend of Robert Eveleigh, Guterma's man of a thousand details and deals. In May, 1957, Eveleigh called Pavis in for a chat. Pavis at the time earned $1,100 a month at Bunge and was the sole support of his wife and five children. The manager of the burlap department testified as to some of the rewards of moonlighting:

PAVIS: Mr. Eveleigh said that there was this company that he thought—that he wanted me to join. He said he thought it presented a very good opportunity; that you never knew how things might go in the business I was in and it might be a good idea, as he put it, to have two strings in your bow.

QUESTION: What company was he talking about?

PAVIS: It developed to be the Commercial Fidelity Corporation [the forerunner of Comficor].

QUESTION: Did he tell you who owned the corporation?

PAVIS: No, sir.

QUESTION: What did he say about its ownership?

PAVIS: He said that it was a privately owned company and that it would be engaged in financial transactions.

QUESTION: Did he outline your duties to you?

PAVIS: He said I would be the president.

Eveleigh went on to assure Pavis that he could continue in his job as manager of the burlap department at Bunge and fulfill his duties as president of Commercial Fidelity Corporation. Pavis accepted the job. Eveleigh's forecast of Pavis' extra workload proved correct. As president, Pavis averaged just several hours of work a week. What was the work he did? he was asked. "Well, the most I ever did," Pavis replied, "was sign documents or checks, minutes, notices of minutes." For these occasional labors he received $500 a month.

As president of Commercial Fidelity Corporation (later Comficor) Pavis was listed as the sole stockholder. According to the records of United States Totalisator, Commercial Fidelity's predecessor, Pavis had been given 80,000 shares of Totalisator's stock in return for the payment of organizational expenses. This stock was supposedly given to Pavis long before he arrived on the scene. The fact that U. S. Totalisator changed its name to Commerical Fidelity Corporation meant that Pavis had become sole stockholder of C.F.C. What made this transaction remarkable was that as president of Commerical Fidelity, Pavis had never purchased or seen a share of the stock he was supposed to own. He was nothing more than a puppet.

This arrangement with Pavis lasted about six months when his superiors at Bunge, his full-time employer, learned through a Dun & Bradstreet report that their burlap department manager was president of an outside firm. Pavis was then asked by a Government attorney whether Eveleigh brought up the name of any other company at the time of his resignation from Commercial Fidelity.

PAVIS: Yes, sir. In the meantime I had been an officer of another corporation.

QUESTION: What corporation did you become an officer of?

PAVIS: The Chatham Corporation.

QUESTION: How did you become an officer of the Chatham Corporation?

PAVIS: One day Mr. Eveleigh said I was an officer in Chatham Corporation.

QUESTION: And what were you? What did he say you were of Chatham?

PAVIS: President.

QUESTION: He told you that you were president of Chatham?

PAVIS: Yes, sir.

QUESTION: What did he tell you about Chatham Corporation when you resigned from Comficor?

PAVIS: Well, I had asked him about that, and he said I couldn't resign from Chatham at the moment, but it would take a little time to work it out and he would let me know, not to be concerned about anything, because there was nothing wrong with Chatham.

Chatham, of course, turned out to be another Guterma holding company. Like Comficor and its predecessor Commercial Fidelity Corporation, Chatham was run by puppets who did Guterma's bidding.

We now come to what has been described as one of Guterma's neater swindles that cost Jacobs about one million dollars. F. L. Jacobs, which the financier controlled, decided it needed to buy some automotive fiber mats. The mats were to be purchased from Classic Carpet Corporation.

Classic was to have a short but interesting history. Formed in December, 1957, Classic operated under its own name for only one week when the company had its name changed. Classic with its new name continued operations as a Jacobs subsidiary. Under the plan worked out, Jacobs would pay for the mats by opening a line of credit in favor of Classic Carpet. This meant that Jacobs went to the Manufacturers National Bank of Detroit and the New York agency of the Swiss Credit Bank and arranged to have Classic withdraw more than one million dollars over a period of time. To put it another way, F. L. Jacobs, using its name and resources, had opened up a one-million-dollar line of credit on which Classic Carpet could draw.

Shortly after Jacobs opened this line or letters of credit for the fiber-mat company, Classic Carpet sold its letters of credit to the pension fund of Sears Roebuck at a discount.

That is, Sears Roebuck paid a little over one million dollars for Classic's line of credit, though it was worth nearly $1,-100,000. This, incidentally, is a normal business procedure which occurs when a company with a line of credit wants to raise cash quickly. Classic, as frequently happens, could only draw on its line of credit at certain future dates, and thus would have to wait for its money.

No sooner had Classic received the one million dollars from Sears Roebuck, then it dealt out the cash to Guterma and his two holding companies. Of the actual sum dispersed, the financier received $66,000, Comficor got $373,000 and Chatham got $250,000. As a result of all this juggling, Jacobs was the loser. When Jacobs, in turn, sold the mats it had purchased from Classic, they brought in no more than $40,-000. In effect, Jacobs by extending the line of credit to Classic had paid one million dollars for these same mats resulting in a loss of $960,000. (One million dollars, the sum Jacobs paid Classic for the mats, minus $40,000 Jacobs received when it sold the mats equals a $960,000 loss.)

What gave the deal its final ironic twist was that Jacobs itself actually owned about half the mats it was supposed to have purchased from Classic Carpet. As Government Attorneys Jerome J. Londin and David P. Bicks later noted in their brief to the United States Court of Appeals, "The fraud is monstrous."

If Guterma had limited himself to Classic Carpet Corporation, he might still be head of Jacobs. But the financier apparently was constitutionally incapable of ignoring the fast deal when opportunity arose. And it appears that as long as Guterma sat at the controls of the auto-parts manufacturer opportunity was invariably present. In fact, it was just such a series of opportunities that in the end were to prove Alexander Guterma's undoing.

Like Birrell, Guterma had a penchant for dealing with moneylenders. According to the Government, Scranton Corporation shares which Jacobs owned were pledged to the lenders for loans and the money received ended up in Guterma's personal holding company. Here is how the scheme worked. Jacobs paid out over two million dollars in cash or through an exchange of assets for 96,900 shares of Scranton. This investment, incidentally, amounted to about 30 per cent of Jacobs' net worth. The Jacobs-owned shares of Scranton were then given over to the moneylenders as collateral for loans. Approximately $1,700,000 was raised in this manner. This sum was divided up, according to Government witnesses, with nearly one hundred thousand going to Guterma himself, over one million to Comficor and the remaining $543,000 to Jacobs.

It even reached the point where the purchase of stock was financed by the stock itself. Just how this was done was explained by Seymour B. Lipton, an accountant and assistant treasurer of F. L. Jacobs, during his testimony at Guterma's subsequent trial.

QUESTION: You told us that Comficor purchased shares and then pledged them.

LIPTON: Yes, sir.

QUESTION: How did that work? What happened? Will you tell us what transpired in this purchase and rehypothecation?

LIPTON: Yes, sir. I, usually at Mr. Eveleigh's direction, amongst others, would contact specific brokerage houses at various times, various days, and acquire in the name of Comficor or, I believe, Kent Window Corporation—

QUESTION: What was Kent Window Corporation?

LIPTON: Kent Window Corporation was a subsidiary of Comficor.

QUESTION: What did you acquire?

LIPTON: I am sorry, sir. I don't understand your question.

QUESTION: You say you acquired in the name of Comficor, you testified. I interrupted you.

LIPTON: Yes. Stock, common, usually of the F. L. Jacobs Company and Bon Ami stock, Class A, I think sometimes, mostly Class B.

QUESTION: After you purchased the shares of F. L. Jacobs common stock and Bon Ami common stock through stock brokers in the name of Comficor, Incorporated, what were you then instructed to do?

LIPTON: These shares were left on margin with the brokerage houses, that is, a certain amount of it was paid for, 30 per cent or 40 per cent, the balance being due to the brokerage house. At the specific instances, at the request of usually Mr. Eveleigh, this stock was to be picked up from the brokerage house. The balance then due to the brokerage house was to be paid and the shares so picked up were turned over to the moneylenders as collateral for the loans which they made to the company enabling the stockbrokerage houses to be paid off their margin and any of the excesses to go into the company funds.

QUESTION: You mean into Comficor's funds?

LIPTON: Sometimes.

QUESTION: *So that the loans from the moneylenders were used to pay off the margin accounts of Comficor in which they had bought Bon Ami and F. L. Jacobs stock, is that correct? And these shares of F. L. Jacobs were then delivered to the moneylenders as collateral for the loans?*

LIPTON: *Yes, sir.** But this does not only apply to Comficor.

QUESTION: Whom else did it apply to?

LIPTON: Well, there were some F. L. Jacobs company loans.

QUESTION: What did they use as collateral?

* Italics supplied.

LIPTON: I don't recall the exact details, sir. I think Scranton Corporation stock was used.

According to the government, Guterma and his private holding companies would borrow more money than was necessary to pay for the stock purchases by adding Jacobs owned shares of Scranton to the collateral, then pocket the difference. Furthermore, the Government claimed, Comficor and Guterma borrowed large sums of money by pledging their Jacobs stock and then never repaid the loans. As the Federal Government noted in its brief to the U. S. Court of Appeals: "Thus, appellants profited when they stole Jacobs assets and again when they 'borrowed' from the moneylenders against their shares in Jacobs."

To succeed in all this juggling it was necessary that the price of Jacobs shares on the New York Stock Exchange remain high. The reason for this was simple enough. The amount of the loan made by the moneylenders was determined by the market price of the securities used as collateral. For example, if the stock-market price of a certain block of Jacobs stock came to $1,000 the moneylenders would take these shares as collateral or security and then lend the owner $800. The purpose of giving the owner less than the stock was actually worth was to protect the moneylender from a rapidly falling market. Thus, if the stock market price of the Jacobs stock dropped to $900 the lender, if he wished, could sell out and protect himself from any loss. Under such circumstances the borrower could prevent the moneylender from selling the shares by putting up more cash or collateral. Conversely, a rise in the market price of the stock would raise the value of the collateral, which in turn meant that Guterma could borrow more money. And, on occasion, that is precisely what happened.

In one instance an increase in the price resulted in an additional $24,000 advance to Guterma on the same collateral. To put it another way, if the price of the Jacobs stock could be kept high, Guterma and his holding companies would not be forced to put up additional collateral or cash. In fact, if the price of the stock could be increased, it would mean even greater cash advances would be made by the moneylenders to the financier.

To boost the price of the Jacobs stock, Guterma employed a manipulative device known as "painting the tape." His tool again was Comficor. According to the Government, Comficor simply purchased Jacobs stock at the close of the day's trading. The purchase was made at a higher price, causing Jacobs to close on the up side. To hide these manipulations Comficor made purchases through eleven brokerage houses including one in Toronto and another in Philadelphia.

Starting in the fall of 1958, the financier found himself in the position of the performer who had complicated his juggling act to the point where dozens of pins were simultaneously flying through the air. Despite his wizardry, Guterma would lose control and the show would end with a resounding thud.

The first hint of trouble occurred in the summer of 1958 when Ernst & Ernst, Jacobs' accountants for twenty-five years, had difficulty in obtaining the information needed to make the annual audit of Jacobs' books. This annual report was to cover Jacobs' activities for the fiscal year ending July 31, 1958. The report was of extreme importance. According to the S.E.C.'s regulations every company that has securities listed on a registered national exchange must file an annual report within 120 days after the close of the fiscal year. In Jacobs' case the report had to be filed with the S.E.C. and the New York Stock Exchange where Jacobs' stock was traded. The Jacobs' annual report had to include certified balance sheets and a certified profit and loss statement for the fiscal year.

The purpose of filing such reports is to protect those who wish to buy a company's stock. This is one of the ways whereby the investor can find out how well a company is doing.

Despite Ernst & Ernst's conscientious efforts, the huge accounting firm found their work repeatedly obstructed by a series of delaying tactics. The reason, though not apparent to all at the time, was simple enough. In order to conceal his incursions into the Jacobs' treasury, the Government later noted, Guterma could not allow the publication of an annual report that reflected Jacobs' true financial condition.

Eventually patience on the part of Government and Exchange officials began to wear thin. On November 14, one New York Stock Exchange official wrote to the financier requesting the annual report and asking why it had been delayed. Four days later Guterma replied that the accountants and outside auditors were working at full speed and that they would be finished within two to three weeks. On the following day one of the accountants who apparently was unaware that he had been allowed to work with such rapidity wrote to Guterma and Eveleigh informing them that an audit was needed. He further explained that due to the lapse of time the audit could not be certified unless it were expanded to cover the period beyond the end of the fiscal year.

Guterma was in a bind. If he delayed further in having the audit completed, both the S.E.C. and the Stock Exchange would act and all of Guterma's pins would be knocked from his flailing hands. However, if the audit was completed the financier's machinations would be exposed.

In desperation an appeal was made to both the S.E.C. and the Exchange for an extension of time. The S.E.C. granted the request. But the Stock Exchange turned it down. Then, on December 4, 1958, the first major blow against the financier was struck when the New York Stock Exchange announced that it had suspended trading on Jacobs' stock, a move that would automatically depress the price of the holding company's shares. This in turn would mean that the moneylenders who held Jacobs' stock as security would be forced to sell out to protect themselves against a falling market, unless, of course, Guterma could put up either additional cash or more stock. The sequence of events were recalled by Jerry Pressman, partner in the Silver Company which had made a series of loans to Jacobs, Comficor, Chatham and Guterma. It was a crucial day for Sandy Guterma.

"I received a call," Pressman later testified, "from Mr. Guterma's office—I was in Dallas, Texas—that it was important for him to talk to me. I later found out that, while it came from his office, he was in California. He called me to tell me—I don't recall the time, but he called me to tell me that F. L. Jacobs stock was suspended, and in light of the fact that he owed me considerable money he wanted me to know that direct from him that the stock was suspended; and, while I don't recall my exact words, I do recall that we came to a conclusion that we had better meet immediately."

According to Pressman he met with Guterma the next morning, a Friday, in a Beverly Hills or Hollywood hotel.

QUESTION: Did you have a conversation with Mr. Guterma at that time with respect to the loans of Comficor, Mr. Guterma and Mr. Eveleigh?

PRESSMAN: Yes, sir.

QUESTION: And what did Guterma say?

PRESSMAN: When he told me of this particular problem, I called his attention to the fact that they were all demand,* and I am making my demand for all my moneys in light of the fact that the collateral I had had lots of value, that I expected him either to pay it or give me additional collateral satisfactory to my associates and myself.

QUESTION: What did Guterma say to you in response to your demand?

PRESSMAN: He told me he would be unable, with the many problems that he was faced with—he would be unable to pay me that particular day, but he hoped that, if I gave him a day or two to think it over, he might come up with a plan that he hoped would meet with my approval."

One plan offered by Guterma was to enlist the aid of Benjamin C. Cohen, president of Reldan Trading Corporation, also a high rate moneylender. Cohen was in California the Friday that Pressman called. The conversation between Cohen, Guterma and Pressman was later recorded in testimony given by Cohen: "Mr. Pressman was concerned about the loans outstanding secured by—which he held— secured by stock of the F. L. Jacobs Company. And the stock having been suspended from trading he complained to Mr. Guterma that he was going to have a problem with the banks because they might call the loans on him or they

* As demand loans they could be called at any time.

had already called the loans on him, and was in a very precarious situation."

According to Cohen, Guterma asked him to take over Pressman's loans or lend some money to Pressman in order that the series of loans be kept afloat. Cohen said that at the time he had outstanding loans made to Comficor with Jacobs as collateral. Cohen said he would help Pressman providing certain conditions could be met. The chief condition was explained by Cohen: "Mr. Pressman was to furnish us with a financial statement indicating net worth in excess of one million dollars, not including the loans secured by Jacobs or Scranton stock." According to Cohen this statement was not forthcoming.

At 9:30 A.M. on the following Monday Pressman again met Guterma, this time in the financier's New York office. The meeting apparently was brief. According to Pressman, Guterma was unable to give him additional collateral and he was unable to make any payments. Pressman replied that he had no other choice but to liquidate as quickly as he could. Jerry Pressman was then asked if Guterma objected to the liquidation plans. "Very seriously," he replied. "Violently is the correct word." That day or the next, the Silver Company began selling Jacobs' stock.

It would appear that the end was indeed near. If Guterma could not halt the sale of the securities of the companies he controlled he could be accused by the S.E.C. of failure to register a secondary offering, a serious charge. Further, the dumping of Jacobs' stock would decrease the value of the holding company and its subsidiaries, a fact which would make the auditors' report appear even less attractive. For the financier there remained only one way by which he could hope to keep the huge balloon from collapsing, and that was to arrange for a large infusion of cash. He was in fact able to raise a great sum in the most daring swindle of his career. The man he indirectly robbed was the late Dominican dictator, Generalissimo Rafael Leonidas Trujillo Molina.

This Guterma operation began innocently enough shortly before the New York Stock Exchange suspended trading in F. L. Jacobs. The financier at the time had prevailed upon an attorney by the name of Saul S. Nevins to serve as a "deal finder," or business "broker." He had been assigned by Guterma to raise capital by finding someone who wanted to buy or invest in the available assets of F. L. Jacobs and its subsidiaries. Nevins later was asked if he could recall some of the people with whom he had preliminary discussions.

"Oh, yes," he said. "Someone who was supposed to be close to Batista, whose name I don't know right now. I had them with Junco [a friend and business associate of Nevins]. I had them with a gentleman who is supposed to be one of the three financial advisers of Mr. Peron. I had them with a Mr.—— I can't think of the gentleman's name, he is an American, and was very close to Mr. Batista. . . ."

Nevins apparently made little progress in his attempts to interest the two deposed dictators in investing in the Guterma empire. However, some time during November or early December, 1958, Nevins met Porfirio Rubirosa, then Dominican Ambassador to Cuba. Rubirosa informed Nevins he would contact one of the lawyer's associates if he could find someone who would be interested in the "deal finder's" propositions. For about one month no communication was forthcoming. Finally in January Rubirosa suggested that a meeting be held in the Caribbean.

On January 31, 1959, two months after the Stock Exchange's suspension of Jacobs, Alexander Guterma flew down to Ciudad Trujillo, then the capital,* where Rubirosa introduced him to Otto Vega, assistant to the President of the Dominican Republic. Vega was to act as the go-between and chief negotiator for his government. The object of the Dominican's interest was the Mutual Broadcasting System which Guterma controlled through the corporate chain that ended at F. L. Jacobs. As a matter of fact, the financier had recently become president of the radio network while his associate Hal Roach Jr. served as chairman of the board. Vega himself later testified as to why Mutual seemed the most promising venture.

VEGA: They [Guterma and Roach] said they were in position to secure here in the United States an outlet for our news, local news down there; that it would be an ideal means of conveying our [Dominican] news here [in America]. To that effect he [Guterma] talked at length about Mutual.

QUESTION: You are talking about Mr. Guterma?

VEGA: I am talking about Mr. Guterma. He talked at length about the advantages of Mutual as the news medium. He showed me a map of the United States showing the location of all their stations in the network.

QUESTION: By them you mean Mutual Broadcasting System, is that right?

VEGA: Mutual Broadcasting System. Mr. Guterma said, "Look, we have 430"—or I may be wrong five one way or the other—he said, "We have some 430 [affiliated] stations throughout the United States; you can look at them on this map. So the news that goes over M.B.C. [sic] really goes over and you have a wide coverage." So he said they were in position to enter into a contract with the Dominican Republic to release here [in the United

* Santo Domingo, its original name, has been restored.

States] our news. . . . We entered into what we might call preliminary talks and the offer was agreeable to the [Dominican] Government in principle.

QUESTION: What was the offer? Can you give it more specifically than that?

VEGA: Yes, sir. He [Guterma] said, "We will give you so many minutes"—I don't recall exactly how many minutes—he said, "We will give you so many minutes over our network for the release of your news items."

QUESTION: What type of news was this to be?

VEGA: Strictly legitimate news concerning the Dominican Republic and its Government, and mostly news concerning our— and when I say our I mean we in the Dominican Republic—our fight against communism. That was the main object.

The proposal must have sounded tempting. For some time the Dominican Government had been trying to mollify a large segment of the American public which was possessed of a dim view of the Caribbean dictator's regime. Then in the winter of 1959 along came a man who had already accomplished much and was now offering to place in the hands of Generalissimo Trujillo the equivalent of a loudspeaker in nearly every American home. It was an abundance of propaganda riches that the Dominican Government could hardly ignore. All that was needed was some small proof that Guterma could deliver what he promised. A showman with a gift for the dramatic, Alexander Guterma would perform the stunt with a single phone call.

According to Vega's own testimony, the financier offered to make a long-distance telephone call while Rubirosa, Vega and Roach remained nearby. "Okay," Guterma said, "I will put in a call to Washington. Give me an idea, some piece of news you would like to broadcast." Otto Vega said he had nothing to offer. "Well," declared Guterma, "since we have Mr. Rubirosa here and Mr. Roach here, why not say Mr. Rubirosa is going to make a picture for Hal Roach Jr., in the Dominican Republic and they are negotiating that." On February 1, 1959, just twenty-four hours later, the make-believe item was carried by Walter Winchell over the Mutual network.*

It was some time during this visit on the weekend of January 31-February 1 that Guterma presented the details of the proposals in an undated letter which he signed as president of Mutual Broadcasting System. The letter was addressed to Otto Vega. The proposal, simply stated, called for Mutual to provide a minimum of broadcast time of news to be furnished by the Dominicans. For this service the Dominican Government in turn would pay Mutual $750,000. Payment would be made in the form of a check to be deposited to the account of Mutual in the Bank of Montreal in Montreal, Canada. Guterma, however, wrote in the margin "if possible in cash which should be much preferred." Finally, and most important, the proposal contained a secrecy clause which stated that the entire transaction was not to be disclosed to anyone not connected with the Dominican Republic "and most certainly to no one in our organization." Thus, it was emphasized in the clearest terms that no one employed by Mutual was to be told about the arrangement.

On February 1—a Sunday afternoon—Guterma and his associates returned to New York in a private plane. The financier had been in the Dominican Republic for approximately forty-eight hours. During the trip back, however, a

---

* It should be noted that there was no reason for Winchell or the Washington staff of Mutual to question the authenticity of the story. Who in his right mind could conceive that the president of a radio network would consciously file a false news item to be used by his own organization? But then no one at that time had begun to reckon fully with Alexander Guterma.

problem arose which opened an unseemly hole in the plan. Guterma showed Nevins the proposal addressed to Vega and asked the lawyer what he thought about it. Nevins said he read it very carefully, adding:

I then told Mr. Guterma that I did not want to have anything to do with the deal that was outlined in that particular letter. And he asked me why not. And I told him that although I have no opinion concerning the legality or illegality concerning the transaction described in that letter, it was nevertheless my experience, my opinion that any parties to a contract of that nature would have to comply with the provisions of the Federal Act requiring registration of foreign agents. . . .

Mr. Guterma indicated to me that he could not understand any requirement that would require registration as a foreign agent because this particular contract was not with a foreign government; it was with an individual. . . . We discussed the matter at some length. I said, as a matter of fact, I know very little about Federal Communications and/or any of the regulations of the F.C.C., which would affect transactions by radio networks. And I was told, not by him [Guterma] but by Mr. Hal Roach that the F.C.C. had no jurisdiction over networks and their jurisdiction extended only to individual radio stations.

I did not choose to argue with him on that particular matter, but indicated that if the facts concerning this transaction became known to the Federal Government there would be no doubt in my mind that they would find some way of bringing a network within their jurisdiction merely because of individual stations being involved. But at any rate I made it very clear that I had no opinion concerning the legality or illegality of the transaction in question other than my opinion concerning the requirement for registration. I also emphasized that it had been more than a year since I had looked at that particular statute, the last time in connection with determining someone else's requirements to register as a foreign agent. And I therefore said that I hesitated in being too definite concerning my opinion. And I certainly would prefer looking into it a little further after reading the actual statute.

Mr. Guterma said to me that by all means I should do so, and that I was to try to figure out some way of having this transaction handled in a legal manner.

Nevins found that after rereading the Foreign Agents Registration Act that his advice to Guterma had proved correct. If Guterma's original proposal had become a binding contract, Mutual, a well-known American company, would have found itself in the quixotic position of having to register as a foreign agent. However, the attorney offered a possible solution whereby Mutual and Guterma could abide by the law and at the same time avoid the necessity of registration as a foreign agent. According to the lawyer the solution was to form a new corporation with the power to act as a bona fide news service. Such a news service engaged in journalist activities would be exempt from registration.

Guterma apparently was satisfied with Nevins' opinion. For on February 2, the financier instructed the lawyer to form a company which was to be called Radio News Service Corporation. Nevins wasted no time. On that same day he called another lawyer in Albany, New York, and instructed him to file a certificate of incorporation. The corporation was duly formed with the Albany attorney and two dummies serving as incorporators. Meanwhile Nevins, who remained in the office of F. L. Jacobs, dictated a new agreement between the Government of the Dominican Republic and Radio News Service Corporation for the dissemination of "news."

Three days later Guterma returned to the Dominican Republic where he presented to Vega the proposed contract with Radio News Service Corporation, telling the Dominican official that this was a wholly owned subsidiary of

Mutual. Under the proposal Vega or those he designated would provide so-called "news" concerning the Dominican Republic to Radio News Service which, in turn, would relay the news to Mutual. One of the more startling clauses was that Mutual "is under obligation to transmit" the items it received from Radio News Service through "its own facilities and those of all radio stations associated and affiliated with said radio network." In other words, Radio News Service was no more than a funnel for Dominican propaganda.

The Dominican Government's position was further protected with the inclusion of this unbelievable clause which simply and effectively excluded any notion of free and unbiased reporting:

> It is further understood and agreed that we will not transmit any news from any source which in your [Otto Vega's] sole discretion may be inimical to or inconsistent with what you, in your sole and exclusive judgment, may consider to be in the best interest of the people of the Dominican Republic or its Government or those responsible for its policies and orientation.

The contract also stated that news or commentaries mentioning the Dominican Republic would total approximately seven hours or 425 minutes per month and would be made available to the network's subscribers. As in the initial draft, a secrecy clause was included. For all these considerations, the Dominican Republic would pay $750,000 to cover an eighteen-month period. But unlike the original proposal nothing was said about depositing the funds in a Montreal bank. In fact, the pay-off was marked with the Guterma touch.

Upon signing the agreement, Otto Vega dutifully handed

over to Guterma three quarters of a million dollars in cash, most of it in American currency and most of it in one thousand dollar bills. The financier who received the money at his suite at the El Embajador Hotel in Ciudad Trujillo counted two or three stacks, then said, "This will be enough." Fittingly, Vega had brought the money in a plain cloth bag, like a miniature laundry bag, with a string around the top.*

What made the entire scheme so improbable was that the Dominicans actually believed that Guterma could deliver an American radio network. However, it wasn't long before Vega discovered that he had signed a meaningless piece of paper.

Robert F. Hurleigh, then vice president of Mutual, testified that between February and May, 1959, the Washington office received teletypes containing so-called "news" items from the Dominican Republic. Some of the cables were signed by Otto Vega. Hurleigh added, "The news stories which were mailed to us at the outset had on the envelope the name of Ist Von Zeigler, or the opposite [sic]." None of these items, he declared, was broadcast by Mutual.

Toward the end of February Vega began reading reports in the newspapers about Sandy Guterma's operations involving F. L. Jacobs. "When I saw that in the papers," he added, "I said I had better go up to New York and talk to Mr. Guterma and see where we stand, which I did. I came up on the 25th or the 26th [of February] and I talked to him in New York City and with Mr. Roach, and they were in finan-

---

* Guterma later claimed he had been obliged to pay $170,000 in brokerage fees including $25,000 to Vega. Vega, however, denied receiving it. The remaining sum was reportedly rushed to a moneylender. But apparently the money came too late and Guterma was unable to bail himself out.

cial difficulties. He said, 'You have nothing to worry [sic]; we have signed the contract with you and we will do it; just keep on sending the news. This other business has nothing to do with this.' "

Then, on May 16, Vega invited Hurleigh to the Dominican Republic. It was festival time and Hurleigh expected to enjoy a few days of relaxation. Shortly after he arrived Vega inquired about the arrangement involving Radio News Service, Mutual and the Dominican Republic. Hurleigh, unaware of what the network was supposed to have been doing for the last three and a half months, was understandably shocked. Vega was later asked by Referee Asa Herzog during a bankruptcy hearing involving Mutual Broadcasting about his reaction to Hurleigh's ignorance of the entire affair.

HERZOG: You parted with three-quarters of a million dollars in cash; you got a couple of tapes* which were not satisfactory, according to your testimony, because they were not what you sent; then the vice president comes down and he knows nothing at all about the contract. Didn't you have a scene with him, a blowup, didn't you raise the devil with him?

VEGA: With Mr. Hurleigh?

HERZOG: Yes.

VEGA: I believe what he told me he knew about this. "This must be a Guterma affair of which I had no knowledge."

---

* Recordings of broadcasts mentioning the Dominican Republic. Guterma sent tapes of two network broadcasts to Vega to show that the contract was being fulfilled. Actually, both broadcasts, originated by Guterma, involved interviews with a United States Congressman and a U. S. Senator. Both were legitimate news items. One other broadcast, initiated by Nevins before the contract was signed, was a story reporting anti-Batista sentiment in the Dominican Republic. The item, broadcast twice, also was a legitimate news story with both the Associated Press and the United Press sending out similar reports. The total amount of air time involving these four broadcasts came to approximately four minutes.

At the bankruptcy hearing previously mentioned the Dominican Republic attempted to retrieve the $750,000 from the network. However, according to Referee Herzog there was no evidence that Mutual received one penny of the money. He also denied the Dominican Republic's claim on the grounds that Mutual did not perform the contract. Referee Herzog continued in the most forthright language to damn the whole sordid affair:

There is, moreover, further ground to expunge the claim. The plain purpose of the entire transaction was to get the propaganda on the airwaves. In the process, Mutual, while not a contracting party, was to be the unwitting tool. Vega relied on Guterma's connection with Mutual to get the free use of its facilities.

Vega is articulate, intelligent and speaks impeccable English. He was quite aware of the laws relating to registration of foreign agents. The proposal submitted to him intended that Mutual be the contracting party. Yet the abrupt change from Mutual to Radio News Service did not disturb him. I cannot believe that he did not know that the change was made to evade the registration laws. He says he asked Guterma if the contract could be construed as a breech of "your" laws and was satisfied with Guterma's statement: "Let me handle my end of it."

Vega knew that the contract had a "secrecy" clause which would, of course, be utterly meaningless if Mutual registered as a foreign agent. Furthermore, without protest, he paid over $750,-000 in cash, thus facilitating concealment of the existence of the contract and when asked by me why he did this, he responded: "Frankly, I have nothing to say."

(Herzog went on to note that the purpose of the Foreign Registration Act was not to deprive the American people of political information, even if it be the propaganda of a foreign principal, but to bring the activities of such people out into the open and to make known the source and who was paying for it.) He then concluded:

> While the contract in question may not have been illegal per se, it was nevertheless entered into with the deliberate design and intent to defeat the declared public policy of the United States. . . . In the case sub judice, I am convinced that claimant [the Dominican Republic] combined and conspired with Guterma and Roach to spread foreign propaganda in the U.S. without publicizing the nature thereof in plain violation of 612 of Title 22 U.S.C. (Foreign Agents Registration Act) and to defy public policy . . .*

Referee Herzog's decision, delivered on November 5, 1959, came nine months after Guterma's fortunes began their downhill turn. Actually the financier's last corporate breath was drawn, unknown to him, eight months earlier, when the S.E.C.'s Bill Moran received a phone call from a nameless informant on a late Monday afternoon. The informant reported that a Dutch moneylender had begun selling F. L. Jacobs' stock. There was no question in either the mind of Moran or Windels that their mysterious caller was well acquainted with Guterma's operations. The information the informant had supplied called for immediate action.

The next morning Windels ordered sixty S.E.C. investigators and lawyers into the Street to seek out the details of every transaction involving Jacobs' stock that had taken place

---

* Guterma and several of his associates were indicted by a Federal Grand Jury on September 1, 1959, and were charged with violations of the registration provisions of the Foreign Agents Registration Act. During the middle of the third day of the trial Guterma interrupted the proceedings and pleaded nolo contendere or no contest to one count in the indictment. The plea was accepted by the Court over the objections of the Government. On July 18, 1960, Guterma made a motion to withdraw his plea. The motion was denied and on November 2, 1960, the financier was sentenced to eight months to two years in prison and fined $10,000. Subsequently Guterma filed a notice of appeal from the order denying his motion. At this writing that appeal is still pending.

during the preceding months. By Wednesday the S.E.C. had gathered enough information to suspend all trading in Jacobs' stock.* On Friday, February 13, "Black Friday" as Guterma now recalls the day, the tempo of events beat even more swiftly. On that day Guterma resigned all offices he held with Jacobs' and its subsidiaries. Meanwhile, Windels had learned that reservations had been made in the names of the financier and his chief aide, Robert Eveleigh, on a Pan American flight to leave on Sunday, the destination Istanbul, Turkey. Windels obtained a warrant for Guterma's arrest. The warrant was based on what seemed to be a series of minor technical charges, that the financier had failed to file certain required forms with the S.E.C. listing the sale of Jacobs' stock. With Federal agents searching all his known haunts and standing by at every airport, Sandy Guterma voluntarily surrendered the next morning to Federal Judge Sidney Sugarman who released the financier on $5,000 bail after rejecting the Government's plea that bail be set at $100,000. It was Valentine's Day. Guterma, his movements restricted to the New York area, angrily denied that either he or Eveleigh knew anything about Sunday's reservations for Istanbul. "This is the biggest outrage by publicity hounds I've even seen," he declared. "This is getting a man for spitting on the sidewalk."

In a way the financier had a point. Before Guterma had attracted the S.E.C.'s attention, anyone who had failed to file the required monthly or annual financial statements and reports with the Commission could expect at the worst to be brought before a civil court. The penalty, if convicted,

---

* The New York Regional Office was backed up in this probe by a task force from the Special Investigations Unit and the General Counsel's office which flew from Washington to New York to participate in the investigation.

could be no more than an injunction, which simply forbids further violations of the rules. There would be no jail sentence since this could only result from a criminal, not a civil action. But Guterma's so-called "technical violations" (failure to file financial reports) gave Windels the opening for which he had so patiently waited. For these seemingly harmless violations were, the Government said, deliberately committed by the financier to hide a substantial fraud, which, ironically, was not in itself a Federal offense.

On March 16, 1959, a little more than a month since the anonymous informant had called Bill Moran, a Federal Grand Jury backed up Windels' warrant by returning a criminal indictment consisting of twenty-one counts of which nineteen involved Guterma. Also named as defendants were Robert Eveleigh, Comficor and Chatham. The heart of the indictment was that the defendants had conspired to defraud the United States Government by "impeding, impairing, obstructing and attempting to defeat the lawful functions" of the S.E.C. by failing to file required financial reports for Jacobs. The total penalties that could be leveled against Guterma came to $160,000 in fines and thirty-five years in jail.

The trial got under way on December 7, 1959, and lasted for eight weeks. Over fifty witnesses were called. The voluble Guterma, however, never testified. On January 27, 1960, a jury of eleven men and one woman began their deliberations. Exactly two hours later the jury returned with its verdict. Guterma was found guilty on sixteen counts, Eveleigh on thirteen. Also adjudged guilty were Comficor and Chatham, the financier's personal holding companies.

U. S. District Judge Lloyd F. MacMahon, who presided, set the sentencing for February 17. Before announcing the penalties, the judge asked Guterma if there was anything he wished to say in his own behalf. In the only words he ever spoke in court the financier replied:

"Your Honor, I believe Mr. Wels [Guterma's attorney] has stated exactly what is in my mind. I have very little to say, except to say I realize that I have been found guilty of violating certain Securities and Exchange Regulations.

"I did not loot the Jacobs company. I did not bilk it of its assets. If there is a shrinkage in Jacobs' assets of three and a half million dollars as shown in the balance sheet, it does not reflect the disappearance of any assets, it reflects a writedown of assets that are present and existing.

"I know it is not proper for me to go into the details of the case. I merely mention this to your Honor because there have been articles in the press stating that three and a half million dollars are missing. That three and a half million dollars is three and a half million dollars that represents a write-off of Scranton stock and other assets on the books of F. L. Jacobs Company.

"Mine is the first case, as Mr. Wels said, of its kind being tried. It is not like the captain of a ship who rammed the Staten Island Ferry on a sunny day. If I am guilty of the offenses, your Honor, I find myself as a mariner befogged in a sea of governmental regulations, and perhaps in the eyes of the law I am guilty, but I didn't do it willfully, I didn't do it knowingly, and I certainly did not do it for any personal gain or benefit because I have no money, I have lost my entire fortune in the Jacobs Company.

"That is all I have to say, your Honor."

Judge MacMahon's reply was brief. He sentenced Guterma to four years and eleven months in prison and fined him $160,000. He gave Eveleigh two years and eleven months and a $10,000 fine. Comficor received $120,000 in fines and Chatham, $10,000.

The financier, however, did not give up. He appealed his conviction to the United States Court of Appeals which dismissed two of the charges against him and lowered his fine to $140,000. The Court also dismissed one of the charges against Eveleigh. However, no change was made in the jail sentences meted out to both men. Guterma then appealed to the United States Supreme Court which declined to review the case, meaning the Court of Appeals decision was allowed to stand. Thus, for the first time since Congress had passed the Securities laws failure of a company to file the required financial reports with the S.E.C. had ended in a criminal conviction. Ironically, Alexander Guterma could claim responsibility for one of the most important judicial decisions in the history of the Commission.

Many people have attempted to explain the rise and fall of Alexander Guterma. Perhaps the financier himself summed it up best when he had printed the following quotation on a card that he gave to his friends. The message was headed "Uncalculated Risk."

One of Webster's cartoons that sticks in the memory pictures the end of a bridge game. A bystander is solemnly reproving the winning couple and saying, "You wouldn't have won if you had played it right."

You can almost elevate that remark to the rank of an axiom that those who have made the greatest achievements of history would not have won if they had "played it right." That is, they would not have won if they had observed all the rules of caution and prudence and made a careful calculation of probabilities.

This is true not only of history but of your own life. Your marriage, for instance. The chances are that if you had played it right, you would not have married when you did. You couldn't afford it while you were getting only $1000 a year, with a good chance of getting fired next month. You were just a couple of babes in the woods. But what lovely woods! And in the end, you won!

The same is true of babies. If a couple waits until the absolute right time to have a baby, they find there *is* no convenient time. There never was. The greatest Baby of all was born at a very inconvenient time: the parents were on a journey; there was no room for them in the inn. If parents play it absolutely right, with 100 per cent caution, they never win.

"A bird in the hand is worth two in the bush" is the motto of all the cowards in the world. If there is to be any winning there must be risk.

—"Simeon Stylites" in *The Christian Century*.

Compliments of ALEXANDER L. GUTERMA

6. THE HERO IS A SCOUNDREL

A few days after the week end of July 4, 1958, the Pittsburgh newspapers reported the abrupt disappearance of an extraordinarily self-assured young man. What made Earl Belle appear so self-confident could have been explained by a series of unusual accomplishments. Between the ages of twenty-four and twenty-six he had: left four banks in an uproar, participated in an artful stock manipulation on the nation's second largest exchange and managed to gain control of nine corporations with an annual sales volume of over five million dollars. At the time of his disappearance, however, Belle's reputation was unsullied. He was in fact known as the young financial genius who helped save a small Pennsylvania community from economic ruin. When he was finally located in Rio de Janeiro a few days after the Pittsburgh papers began printing their stories, Earl Belle was already making headlines throughout the United States as the youngest securities fugitive in history.

Belle's entrance into the world of high finance at so early an age can be attributed to a combination of luck and precocity. His own family certainly had neither wealth nor connections. His father had left his butcher shop in McKees-port, Pennsylvania, to sell off-brand shoes. His mother was a teacher in the Pittsburgh public school system.

Shortly after graduating from high school Belle, then eighteen, eloped to Winchester, Virginia, with a girl friend of fifteen. The couple attended the University of Pittsburgh, with Belle specializing in business administration, incidentally the only formal training he received for his later career. The first Mrs. Belle who remained with Earl for about seven years, testified during divorce proceedings that her husband quickly displayed his love for luxuries along with a spirit of contempt for those who served him. She claimed that while she worked as a school teacher, Belle would commandeer her pay checks and put them in a bank account under his name, setting aside only enough money for her lunches. While pinching his wife's pennies, the newly-wed husband dressed in two-hundred-dollar custom-tailored suits. Typically, when traveling by plane he never carried his own suitcase. Instead, he would toss coins to whatever airline personnel might be around, expecting them to pick up his luggage.

Upon graduating from college, Belle might well have counted his assets. They included an ingratiating personality and a fully ripened Machiavellian instinct for the unscrupulous. Wasting no time in getting started, Belle took his first step by renewing his boyhood acquaintance with two brothers, Murray and Burton Talenfeld. Their father, Edward Talenfeld, had become a moderately successful Pittsburgh real-estate man. It was to Edward Talenfeld that Belle made his first proposition. Belle promised the older man he could obtain a 100 per cent mortgage on some property in which Edward Talenfeld was interested. True to his word, Belle produced the mortgage and won an important friend. A few months thereafter Belle came to Edward Talenfeld with still another suggestion. This time he offered Talenfeld an option on a controlling block of stock of the First National Bank of Saltsburg, Pennsylvania. And it was at this point that Belle's operation began in earnest.

Saltsburg was a tiny community (population 1,156) not far from Pittsburgh. Despite its proximity to the city, the town's population was steadily declining. In fact, no new industry had come to the community in the past seventy years. The only hope for Saltsburg's survival would be an infusion of new blood and, most important, new business. Ironically, the town would obtain both as the result of the efforts of Belle and the Talenfelds.

While Edward Talenfeld was acquiring control of the Saltsburg bank the Talenfelds and Belle set up the Eastern Investment and Development Corporation whose main purpose at the time was to engage in the development of real estate and to help the town of Saltsburg. The most important thing they could do, of course, was to bring industry into the community. At the time the Pittsburgh Urban Redevelopment Program was displacing a number of firms in the Pittsburgh area. The Talenfelds and Belle hoped that they could convince one of the companies to come to the nearby town. One of the firms they approached was Steiner Manufacturing Company, a maker of draperies, which was being uprooted from its old site. The drapery manufacturer was willing to make the move if a plant could be provided. The townsfolk were understandably enthusiastic. They banded together and subscribed to a $112,000 public bond issue, the equivalent of $100 for every man, woman and child in Saltsburg. The plant was built by Eastern, the

Belle-Talenfeld development corporation, at a cost of $230,000, the remaining money being put up by district banks. The Steiner factory alone provided 150 desperately needed jobs.

The town of Saltsburg, taking courage in what had been accomplished, turned to Belle and the Talenfelds for further growth. A second plant was constructed for the Jiffy Steak Company, a meat processor, adding more than fifty jobs. The third and final acquisition was a tool manufacturer. While these plants were being built, the town constructed a new school and fire house. As a result Saltsburg won the $3,000 first prize "bootstrap award" given at the annual State Community Improvement Contest. Though the community had done much of the work, the people of Saltsburg owed a large measure of their success to Earl Belle and his young associates who not only sat on the board of directors of Eastern but also of the First National Bank of Saltsburg.

Further praise for Belle and Murray Talenfeld came from the *Eastern Banker* in an article entitled, "The Little Bank That Could, Or The Tale of Two Men of Saltsburg." The periodical noted that the Saltsburg bank was alleviating the community's housing shortage by financing ranch-type homes. Then it declared, "At a time in our economic history when money for investment is at a premium, the effective use of idle bank deposits has resulted in the rebirth of a community that was in danger of perishing. To the necessary source of funds, Belle and Talenfeld have added the human element, sound banking practices and a well thought out program for the administration of these previously unproductive resources. This combination has resulted in an economic comeback for Saltsburg and a role in the community for the bank."

The magazine also mentioned that the two young men had accomplished in less than a year what was thought to be impossible for the past half-century. Belle at the time was twenty-four, and Murray Talenfeld, twenty-three.

There is no doubt that if Belle and his associates had limited their operation to rebuilding Saltsburg and the bank, they would be respected citizens today. However, Belle, who swaggered while others walked, had more ambitious dreams. Brilliant in a business sense, he would eventually help to build a corporate empire with the aid of the Talenfeld brothers. The foundation for this scheme was a company appropriately called Cornucopia Gold Mines.

Cornucopia had once been a silver and gold mining operation with most of its claims located near Cornucopia, Oregon. Incorporated in 1930, the company ceased active operations about one month before Pearl Harbor. The reasons given at the time were increased operating costs coupled with poor mining results. The firm remained dormant during and after World War II, employing just three men and two part-time stenographers and bookkeepers whose major duties were to maintain the mines and equipment with the hope that some day production could be resumed. Though never truly successful—the company paid only one dividend during its entire history and that was three cents a share—Cornucopia had one important asset. It was listed on the American Stock Exchange.

In the beginning of 1957, Kalman Greenhill, a New York attorney and business broker, conferred with Belle and the Talenfelds on Eastern's expansion through the purchase of other companies. After discussing various possibilities, Greenhill introduced them to Abraham A. Franks, a Boston businessman. About two years previously Franks had acquired a little over two million shares of Conucopia stock in exchange for some uranium claims plus a payment of $100,-000. This gave Franks ownership of a little more than half of the nearly 4,000,000 outstanding shares of the dormant gold mining company.

Then, in May, 1957, an agreement was worked out whereby Franks sold to Eastern, the Belle-Talenfeld development firm, one million of the two million shares he owned in Cornucopia. For these shares Eastern agreed to pay $240,000, including two corporate notes totaling $90,000. Franks, in effect, had made a profit of $140,000. In addition, since he had sold only one million shares to Eastern, he still owned another million.

A problem still had to be solved. If Franks's remaining one million shares were sold to the public, a registration statement would have to be filed with the S.E.C. since these were "control" securities. Another agreement was worked out whereby Franks would deposit his one million shares in a voting trust consisting of the three Talenfelds, Belle and Franks. While Franks had only one vote, Belle and the Talenfelds combined had four votes. It would appear, though Franks still owned the one million shares, "control" of Cornucopia had passed out of his hands. Thus, the S.E.C. regulations calling for registration and disclosure had been circumvented, or so it seemed.

The agreement was predicated on one other condition. And now things really get complicated. For every two shares that Franks would sell out of the one million he owned, Eastern would have the right to make Franks buy one of its million shares. To put it another way, if Franks sold two shares at one dollar each, Eastern had the right to make Franks buy one of their shares for seventy-five cents. What all this meant was that if the price of Cornucopia stock should rise and Franks sold his one million shares, Eastern would be able to sell back five hundred thousand shares to Franks at a substantial profit. At the same time it would retain half of the one million shares originally bought from Franks which in turn could be used to buy other companies. Finally, if the price of Cornucopia should increase substantially, the shares Eastern owned would be even more valuable when traded for expansion purposes. As Edward Talenfeld succinctly summed it up: "You can buy more companies with a three-dollar stock than a fifty-cent stock."

The only remaining problem was how to raise the price of Cornucopia stock. Starting on May 1, 1957, there was a sudden burst of activity in Cornucopia on the American Stock Exchange. Bruce Hilsee, one of the S.E.C.'s finest investigators whose detective work was largely responsible for the government's subsequent action, learned that during the first few days of May more shares of Cornucopia were traded than had been traded in all the prior months of 1957. Between May 1 and August 1, a period of three months, the total trading volume for Cornucopia on the American Exchange amounted to 656,400 shares. Prices soared from about 31 cents to 87 cents per share, a two hundred per cent increase.

To find the explanation for this rapid rise, Hilsee searched the various metropolitan newspapers as well as the *Wall Street Journal.* He was looking for favorable news items concerning Cornucopia's activities or prospects which would account for the increase in price and trading. No such news item could be found in the New York papers. He also telegraphed the company's home office in Spokane, Washington. According to the Spokane office there had been no change in Cornucopia's business operations. Meanwhile, Hilsee traveled to Pittsburgh, where the cause for the extraordinary rise in the price of Cornucopia shares became apparent.

His three-day investigation disclosed that approximately twenty-five Pittsburgh residents had purchased more than 100,000 shares of Cornucopia stock. Hilsee discovered that the purchasers had bought Cornucopia as the result of the activities of one or more individuals in control of Eastern. At least 42,000 shares alone were bought by fourteen people, most of them relatives and friends of Belle and the Talenfelds who had recommended that they buy the stock. (One block of 300 shares was purchased by Belle's wife for the account of his personal physician.)

As it turned out several of the substantial purchasers were dummies who did not really own the shares but had been persuaded to appear as the real owners. In fact, some of the money used by one of the dummies to purchase Cornucopia stock came from loans made by the Saltsburg bank.

A detailed study of the trading showed that almost half of the volume on the American Stock Exchange could be attributed to five accounts which in effect were acting for Belle or the Talenfelds. Buy orders were invariably placed in such a manner and time as to influence the price. Brokers were told to buy at the end of the day's trading and thus create a strong closing market price. Brokers were also given a 5,000 to 10,000 share market buy order with instructions to buy in smaller lots. This had the effect of keeping a sustained and stable demand for the stock.

Meanwhile, an attempt was made to get the general public to begin buying Cornucopia stock. Hilsee discovered that the Pittsburgh newspapers themselves were unwittingly be-

ing manipulated to help foster enthusiasm for Cornucopia.
The S.E.C. investigator later reported the following:

Coincident with the increase in trading activity and price of
shares in Cornucopia, the Eastern group embarked on a publicity
campaign regarding its plans and prospects. Their public relations agent, Louis Mendelsohn, caused at least two articles to be
published in the *Pittsburgh Post-Gazette*. According to the financial editors, he delivered at least four "handouts" to the *Pittsburgh Post-Gazette* and the *Pittsburgh Press*. The *Press* published
on May 8, 1957, a lengthy article regarding the Eastern Group.
Edward Talenfeld has stated that these press articles came from
Murray Talenfeld's office. There was one article in the *Eastern
Banker* relative to the Eastern Investment and Development Corporation published in May, 1957. These articles speak in glowing
terms of Eastern Investment & Development Corporation and
Cornucopia. . . .

Still other methods were employed to tell the public about
Cornucopia's promising future. Tannen and Company, a
broker-dealer located in Wall Street, joined in an arrangement to sell Cornucopia stock off the Exchange. These over-
the-counter sales were to be made to the general public. The
off-the-exchange price would be based on the last price
quoted on the Exchange for that day's trading. Tannen, later
closed down by the S.E.C., employed the usual boiler-room
methods of attracting customers, including long-distance
phone calls and brochures containing overly optimistic statements about Cornucopia and its prospects.

Typical was the eight-page brochure mailed to prospective clients which began with this propitious headline in
solid black type: "CORNUCOPIA GOLD MINES . . .
POTENTIAL GIANT IN THE MAKING." After noting
that Eastern controlled the former gold mining company,

the brochure proceeded to describe Eastern and Cornucopia's accomplishments and future in glowing terms. It then listed Cornucopia's five directors. Besides Earl Belle and Murray Talenfeld, others named were Philip C. Gifford, senior partner in a brokerage house and chairman of the board of directors of Wolverine Power Corporation; Barney Keywell, vice president of Hancock Steel Company in Detroit, and Franco Modigliani, full professor, Graduate School of Industrial Administration, Carnegie Institute of Technology and Business Consultant to the office of U. S. Naval Research. Both Belle and Talenfeld were described as bankers and Pittsburgh real estate developers. For the uninitiated investor Cornucopia's new board of directors must have sounded impressive.

One final problem remained. Where would Tannen and Company obtain the shares it was selling to the public? Under the original plan, the broker-dealer was to act as agent for Franks who still owned one million shares. According to S.E.C. regulations stock sold to the public must be registered with the Commission if the shares being sold represent a controlling interest in the company. The Franks shares that Tannen planned to sell, however, had not been registered with the Commission. These shares, as noted previously, had been placed in a five-member voting trust consisting of Franks himself, Belle and the three Talenfelds. Since Franks was neither an officer nor a director of Cornucopia and since he had only one out of five votes, it would appear that the shares were not "control" stock. Franks, however, to make sure that he was abiding by the S.E.C.'s rules, asked the Commission for an opinion on selling the shares without registering them. The Commission in turn told the Boston businessman that appearances to the contrary his one million shares would be considered "control" stock and thus would have to be registered with the S.E.C. if sold to the public.

Tannen meanwhile had already sold about 150,000 shares of stock to the public. As the result of the S.E.C. opinion, Franks, lawfully abiding by the Commission's informal ruling, had refused to make delivery of the shares to Tannen. This meant that Tannen would be unable to deliver to the hundreds of innocent buyers the shares they had agreed to purchase at exorbitant prices which had been set by the manipulation on the Exchange. There was only one solution. The Belle-Talenfeld dummies were forced to turn over to Tannen the shares they had purchased while manipulating Cornucopia on the American Stock Exchange. Belle and the Talenfelds neither lost nor gained from this involved operation. However, the investing public which bought Cornucopia shares from Tannen were cheated out of thousands of dollars through the purchase of artificially inflated stock.

The failure on the part of Belle and his associates to unload all the Cornucopia shares they had hoped to sell forced them to alter their plans. Since Franks had not sold any of his remaining Cornucopia shares he had not purchased the Cornucopia stock held by Eastern, which he would have had to do under the agreement mentioned earlier. These purchases by Franks, if they had been made, would have given Eastern the money it needed to buy up other companies. The result was that Belle and the Talenfelds had to look elsewhere for funds if their empire building dreams were to be realized. The key to these dreams remained unchanged. It was Cornucopia, the still dormant gold mine.

From time to time Belle and the Talenfeld brothers had

been in contact with Kalman Greenhill, the New York business broker who had introduced them to Franks. Greenhill had submitted information on various companies for their consideration but the preliminary negotiations were unsuccessful. Then, in September, 1957, a little more than two months after the manipulation on the American Exchange had ended, Belle or Murray Talenfeld contacted Greenhill again. This time they wanted to know whether a Birmingham holding company called Alabama Acceptance Corporation would be interested in parting with five subsidiaries. They consisted of a printing firm with offices in Deposit, New York; a Pittsburgh water-heater manufacturer; and three Long Island firms including a realty company, an electronics maker and a machine shop. All but one of the subsidiaries was in poor financial condition. The one that had been doing well—the water-heater maker—had just loaned $250,000 to Alabama which it used to finance the operations of its subsidiaries.

Considering the poor financial condition of its subsidiaries the Alabama group found the Belle-Talenfeld offer attractive. Payment for the subsidiaries consisted of about two million newly issued shares of Cornucopia which were to be in a five-man voting trust, three members of which could be named by the Eastern group. The sale was made final on January 27, 1958. Earlier in the month, Cornucopia purchased 80 per cent of the Steiner Manufacturing Company, the drapery maker that had moved to Saltsburg. Payment consisted of $20,000 in cash, six promissory notes totaling $175,000 to be met over a period of six years, and issuance of 405,000 shares of Cornucopia. There were now over 6,500,000 shares of Cornucopia outstanding.

At this point Earl Belle was becoming trapped in the

happy illusion that he was in truth a financial genius whom the public should get to know. To announce his corporate triumphs Belle gave a sumptuous press party in New York, hiring three planes to fly newsmen and prominent civic and business leaders from Pittsburgh. The entertainment offered included a 24-piece string orchestra, the best whiskey and some of the city's loveliest and most knowledgeable hostesses. The $20,000 bill was paid by Eastern Investment and Development Corporation.

Belle himself was no stranger to the good life. He made frequent trips to New York, staying in $100-a-day hotel suites and dining handsomely in Manhattan's most expensive night clubs. When in Pittsburgh, he lived in a $70,000 home, which he purchased with a $5,000 down payment. He entertained lavishly, once chartering two helicopters to take his friends to a picnic. And if anyone in his home community still doubted Belle's success, they need only observe his stable of three cars, a Jaguar, a Mercedes-Benz valued at $5,000 and a white Cadillac. The cars were driven by a chauffeur while the young financier wearing a raccoon coat majestically peered out at the passing scene.

While Belle swaggered around town, the companies purchased from Alabama were already in desperate financial difficulties. Eastern, the parent of Cornucopia, which had served as the original source of capital, was soon drained of funds. Cornucopia itself which owned the Alabama subsidiaries had been dormant for years and thus had little money to begin with. And the Alabama subsidiaries, the hoped-for money makers, were sinking deeper in the red. To keep the operation going it was obvious that there had to be an addition of new funds. Since no bank would loan money if it knew the truth, illusion had to take the place of reality.

One of the first victims was the Security National Bank of Huntington, Long Island. The bank was already involved to the extent that it had outstanding loans to two of the subsidiaries Cornucopia had purchased. Belle and Murray Talenfeld then dropped in on the bank asking for a substantial line of credit. Their trump was a financial statement that showed that Eastern as of July 31, 1957, had a net worth of $1,867,317, a considerable exaggeration. What made the statement acceptable to the bankers was that it bore the signature and letterhead of Myron Swartz and Company, a Pittsburgh certified public accounting firm.

How this came about was later explained by Swartz himself. He and Belle had become acquainted while attending the same high school, their friendship renewed when they both took the same night course at the University of Pittsburgh. One Saturday in the summer of 1957, Belle called Swartz at home and requested that the accountant do some work for him during the following day.

On Sunday Swartz met Belle at the offices of Eastern where Belle requested Swartz to prepare a balance sheet. Swartz did as he was told. That evening Belle informed Swartz that he was leaving for New York that very night and had to take the balance sheet with him. Belle, meanwhile, had glowingly described Eastern's future, adding that Swartz was to be the accountant for the entire business. Swartz, not suspecting any trickery, agreed to give Belle his working papers, his firm's stationery, which was blank except for Swartz's signature and a binder to contain the balance sheet and letter. Belle, in turn, told Swartz that he would have the balance sheet and covering letter typed. Instead, a different statement which raised Eastern's worth was prepared and typed on the blank, signed stationery that Swartz had given Belle. The same procedure also applied to the covering letter which stated that an audit had been made of Eastern's books. Of course no audit had been made, a fact Swartz had originally noted.

Before extending the credit to Belle and Murray Talenfeld, the vice president at the Long Island bank contacted the president of the Peoples Union Bank and Trust Company in McKeesport, a community near Pittsburgh. The Talenfelds had previously obtained from the McKeesport bank an unsecured $50,000 loan which, unknown to both banks at the time, had been made on another erroneous financial statement. The head of the McKeesport bank proceeded to quote figures from this erroneous statement to the vice president of the Long Island bank. These figures supported the recommendation that Eastern's credit was good. The McKeesport banker added that Belle's personal statement showed a net worth of $78,000. With all these assurances the Security National Bank of Long Island granted Cornucopia an unsecured line of credit totaling $200,000. On November 21, 1957, Cornucopia borrowed the full $200,000, much of which was used as operating capital for Cornucopia and its subsidiaries.

This $200,000 loan, however, was not sufficient and by January, 1958, Cornucopia was again seriously in need of cash. To obtain still another loan Belle and Murray Talenfeld invited the vice president and another officer of the Long Island bank to Pittsburgh. If there had been any doubts about how well Eastern, the parent company, was thriving they need only look for themselves.

Upon their arrival in Pittsburgh the bankers were met by Belle and Murray Talenfeld at the city's airport, where they transferred to two helicopters that Earl and Murray had rented for the day. With Belle and one banker in the first helicopter and Murray and the other banker in the second, they proceeded to fly to the site of Eastern's most prosperous venture, the little town of Saltsburg.

Unknown to the bankers, Belle and Murray had hired a battalion of bulldozers, pile drivers and earth-moving machinery. This equipment had been conveniently placed in a field near the Saltsburg ball park. After Belle and Murray directed the bankers' attention to the Steiner Manufacturing plant and about seven ranch houses Eastern had built, the helicopters headed toward the Saltsburg ball park. As the helicopters flew over the nearby field, the workers below busily moved the machinery back and forth while Belle and Murray Talenfeld explained to the bankers that what they were seeing was an integral part of Eastern's operations.

As they flew back to Pittsburgh, Earl and Murray jauntily pointed out to the already wide-eyed bankers other construction sites and buildings in which they actually owned no share but claimed as part of the Eastern complex. Then as the two helicopters swept down over a municipal lot where the city of Pittsburgh stored its heavy construction equipment, Belle leaned out and waved to the workers below. The workers naturally returned the greeting, though they had no idea at whom they were waving. The bankers were left with the impression that this equipment also belonged to Eastern. And from the air, who would believe otherwise?

About a week after the bankers returned to Long Island the National Security loaned Eastern $225,000. The cost to Eastern for renting the helicopters and the construction equipment totaled about $10,000.

Understandably such a stunt could only work once. And

since Eastern, Cornucopia and its subsidiaries were continually in need of funds other means had to be employed to raise the capital. To further encourage the banks to make more loans, Belle promised to bring business to the different institutions by having "friends" deposit large sums. What Belle actually did was to borrow money from one bank and deposit it in others without telling the banks that received the deposits where the money actually came from. To hide the origin of this borrowed money, the banks which received the deposits were tricked into participating in the scheme itself. In fact, without their innocent cooperation the plan would never have worked.

This is what happened. Arrangements were made with a New York money broker to have the Cleveland Trust Company loan $1,600,000 to Eastern. The first loan was for $800,000. This loan was to be made on December 11, 1957. Meanwhile, Peoples Union Bank in McKeesport and Security on Long Island were advised that Eastern had friends who were willing to deposit $400,000 in cash in each bank. The deposits would be made around December 11. The two banks issued Certificates of Deposits, similar to receipts one would receive for depositing money in a savings account. The two $400,000 Certificates of Deposit, in this case receipts for money that had yet to be received, were sent to the Chase Manhattan Bank which served as the correspondent bank for Cleveland Trust (the lender) and Peoples and Security (the recipients of the deposits). Meanwhile, Cleveland Trust forwarded the $800,000 to Chase Manhattan who would hold these funds until Chase received the Certificates of Deposit. Once received by Chase that bank placed $400,-000 in the account of Peoples and an equal amount in the account of Security National.

Neither Peoples nor Security National were aware that this $800,000 was the result of loans negotiated by Eastern with Cleveland Trust. Thus, the origin of the $800,000 in new deposits could well have been "friends" of Belle, which Peoples and Security National had been led to believe.

Similar arrangements were made for two other Cleveland Trust loans totaling an additional $800,000. Eastern, of course, never had any use of the money borrowed from the Cleveland bank. In fact, this scheme cost Eastern more than $26,000 in interest payments, the difference between the 2½ per cent interest Eastern received as the result of the deposits and the 5¼ per cent interest Eastern paid Cleveland Trust for the loans. However, as the result of this and other schemes Eastern and Cornucopia were able to borrow substantial unsecured sums from both the McKeesport and the Long Island banks.

Despite the mounting bank loans, it became apparent to Belle and the Talenfeld brothers that these funds were not sufficient to keep Cornucopia and its subsidiary companies supplied with working capital. Still another method had to be found to raise money.

Starting in December, 1957, Belle began informing creditors that Cornucopia expected a major underwriting of its stock in the near future. A short time later Belle met Ben Eisenberg, a registered representative with McDonald, Holman & Company, a broker-dealer. Belle soon interested Eisenberg in the possibility of a Cornucopia underwriting. Eisenberg, who had no authorization to negotiate such arrangements for McDonald, Holman, was about to join a newly organized broker-dealer firm called George, O'Neill & Company. This new firm was organized in part by George E.

George, a former stockholder of McDonald, Holman & Company.

In February, 1958, after Belle had talked to Eisenberg, the securities salesman approached George on the subject of underwriting Cornucopia. A meeting was then arranged at the Harvard Club in March. Those attending included Murray and Burton Talenfeld, Mr. George, and Donald B. Marron, a financial analyst and a stockholder of George, O'Neill. During the meeting several uncertified financial statements of Eastern, Cornucopia and its subsidiaries were presented to George, who requested that his firm's accountant prepare financial statements of all the companies. This request was refused. Further, Marron, George's financial analyst, and the Talenfelds clashed over the financial statements that had been presented. Finally, Murray and Burton suggested that the Cornucopia underwriting come out at between $5 and $7 per share, a price which George considered unjustified by the company's current and projected earnings. George declined to participate in the underwriting.*

After the discussion had ended Murray and Burton Talenfeld handed Eisenberg a letter which Eisenberg took to be an underwriting agreement between Cornucopia and McDonald, Holman, the broker-dealer where Eisenberg had once worked. The Talenfelds asked Eisenberg to sign the agreement on behalf of McDonald, Holman. According to Eisenberg he refused because he lacked the authority and also because no agreement was either formulated or discussed. Hugh McDonald, president of McDonald, Holman, reaffirmed later in an affidavit that no underwriting agreement with Cornucopia had been considered or executed.

---

* Belle had been away on his second honeymoon while the discussion with George had taken place and thus had not participated.

Then, around April 1, Murray and Burton Talenfeld visited the Security National Bank. It was late in the afternoon when they arrived. They showed a purported underwriting agreement between Cornucopia and McDonald, Holman to one of the vice presidents of the bank. Five days previously this bank official had met the Talenfelds at McDonald, Holman and was given the impression that the broker-dealer had agreed to the underwriting. After receiving the purported agreement from Murray and Burton Talenfeld at the bank, this officer showed it to two other vice presidents and a director. The Talenfeld brothers indicated the agreement was confidential and that they did not wish to leave it behind. Because of the lateness of the hour, the agreement was not copied. On the basis of this purported agreement, the bank's loan committee agreed to lend Cornucopia $250,000. This brought the total amount borrowed from the Long Island and McKeesport banks to over $800,-000.

At about this time Belle and the Talenfelds had a falling out for some unknown reason. On the night of April 8, shortly after his return from his honeymoon, a warrant was sworn out for Belle's arrest. The warrant charged him with embezzlement. In a quick counterstroke Belle ordered a detective agency to seize physical control of the offices of Cornucopia and Eastern. This was done the following day with the Talenfelds barred from the offices until an agreement, dated April 11, was signed. Starting on the morning of April 10, a separation meeting that lasted twenty hours took place. Immediately after it was signed, Belle and the Talenfelds were busily changing its terms. A final agreement was reached on May 14. In effect, control of the foundering empire, including Cornucopia, had shifted to Belle.

Belle's only hope to save Cornucopia and its subsidiaries from total failure—they somehow couldn't seem to make money—was to hold a stockholders' meeting. At the meeting the stockholders would be called on to approve an increase in Cornucopia's capitalization as well as the authorization of additional shares of stock. The sale of this new stock would then provide the funds so desperately needed by Cornucopia and its subsidiaries.

Before such a meeting could be held, Cornucopia, under the Securities laws, had to submit the proposed proxy statement it would send to its stockholders. However, delay followed delay. Then, on May 20, the American Stock Exchange suspended trading in Cornucopia stock. The company had failed to file its annual report with the Exchange. On May 29 the annual report and the preliminary proxy statement were filed with the Commission. The S.E.C., as the result of the delays, began an investigation of Cornucopia.

Still further complications arose when Alabama, the original holding company that controlled Cornucopia's subsidiaries, was declared bankrupt. On June 16, the Referee in Bankruptcy questioned the legality of the option contract whereby Cornucopia received the right to purchase the Alabama subsidiaries in exchange for Cornucopia stock. During this period the New Jersey state banking examiners began questioning the loans made to Belle, Cornucopia, Eastern and the subsidiary concerns by the Manufacturers' Bank of Edgewater. Belle had previously gained control of the Edgewater bank through a straw man. He had caused the bank to make loans totaling $150,000 to himself and others. After examining the books at Edgewater, the banking examiners requested the president of the bank to remove the loans because they had been made to persons located outside the State of New Jersey.

While the S.E.C. pressed its investigation of Belle and the proxy statement, much of which turned out to be fraudulent, the young financier made the ultimate decision, one which would result in his becoming a fugitive.

During the week of June 23, and unknown to government investigators, Belle called an official of the Saltsburg bank and requested that the bank have a large amount of cash on hand for the following week. On July 3 Belle arrived at the bank with a check payable to Schutter, one of the Cornucopia subsidiaries. The Schutter check came to $40,000. Belle deposited this check into the subsidiary's account at the Saltsburg bank. He then withdrew $40,000 from the Schutter account by writing a check payable to Cornucopia. He followed the same procedure again, withdrawing $40,000 from Cornucopia and then depositing it in Eastern's account. Finally he wrote one more check for $40,000, this one on Eastern's account. He then had the bank official cash the check together with another for $2,000. Both checks were payable to Earl Belle.

The bank official later recalled that during this rather strange proceeding Belle informed him that he was about to visit "friends" of his at the S.E.C. in Washington and that they would help him lift the suspension of trading in Cornucopia stock. During the conversation Belle implied that he needed the cash to bribe someone in the Commission.

The bank official turned over an additional $25,000 in cash to Belle plus a bank check for $17,000. Belle was to cash the check at another bank. However, he could not get to the bank in time and that night the bank official brought Belle

$17,000 and took back the check. Sometime during the July 4th weekend, Belle, who of course had no intention of going to Washington, fled with his new wife, a former New York model, to Rio de Janeiro. He was accompanied by Mitchell Ostwind, a young associate who had helped him in various affairs including the take-over of the Edgewater bank. When S.E.C. investigators called on Belle's Pittsburgh office a few days later, all they found were eight telephones, a box filled with financial records and two bewildered secretaries.

Federal and state officials began the dismal task of totaling the losses left in the wake of Earl Belle's departure. The Security National Bank of Long Island was forced to write off $475,000 in loans. The Peoples Union Bank of McKeesport began a battle to recover $200,000 in another unsecured loan. The Manufacturers' Bank of Edgewater, New Jersey, was permanently closed by the New Jersey State Banking Commission. The bank which had only $130,000 in capital had given Belle and others $150,000 in fraudulent loans. In addition, Eastern, Cornucopia and all but one of the subsidiaries ended in bankruptcy. Total losses have been estimated at two million dollars.

Meanwhile, Mitchell Ostwind voluntarily returned to the United States and was subsequently tried for his part in the ruin of the Edgewater, New Jersey, bank. Found guilty, his one-year sentence in a Federal prison was reduced to four months. Also found guilty at the trial were the bank president who received a suspended sentence and a director appointed by Belle who was given nine months, later reduced to three months.

A similar fate awaited the Talenfeld brothers. On August 2, 1961, they pleaded guilty to thirteen charges and no defense to twenty-five other counts. Federal Judge Rabe F.

Marsh in Pittsburgh sentenced each to one year in prison and fined them both $20,000. In handing down his sentence, Judge Marsh said he was fairly certain that Belle was the mastermind of all the illegal stock transactions. Then, commenting on the Talenfeld brothers, he added, "They may have been dupes but they were greedy dupes."

Edward Talenfeld, Murray's and Burton's father, pleaded no contest to three indictments. He received a $7,500 fine, a suspended jail sentence and was placed on five-years' probation.

Belle, at this writing, remains in Rio. Like Birrell, should he return to the United States, he would be forced to stand trial on a series of indictments. However, Belle, if he wishes, can probably take up permanent residence in Brazil. Shortly after his arrival, his second wife gave birth to a baby boy. If the new extradition treaty should be ratified and made retroactive, Belle, as the parent of a Brazilian child, need not fear expulsion.

The only thing that would probably force the young financial fugitive back to the United States would be a severe case of personal bankruptcy. According to Ostwind, such an event seems unlikely. Belle's former associate has said that Earl Belle traveled to Rio with $800,000. Though Belle has told reporters in Brazil that he came with little funds, he is reported to have launched his South American career by renting a $450-a-month penthouse apartment overlooking Copacabana beach. Until recently he was residing there with his family and three butlers. Those gullible enough to listen have heard Belle describe plans to buy a rundown Copacabana restaurant and turn it into an exclusive night club with "international entertainment." He is also supposed to have entered a stock-selling operation, attracting American and Brazilian investors with sumptuous dinners consisting of roast pig, beef, turkey, chicken, shrimp and the finest wines. When his penthouse became too small for these affairs, he reportedly advertised in Rio's English-language newspaper seeking "to rent an apartment or house with nine rooms and private swimming pool, all possible luxuries—money no object."

The concluding note was composed by Belle himself shortly after he arrived in Brazil's most luxurious city. In identical letters to the F.B.I., the United States Attorney in Pittsburgh, three banks which he had left in an uproar and five newspapers, Belle declared:

"I am deeply sorry for all the people who have been misled and for all the wrongs done and for the unwitting part I played in the deception. I wanted so much to succeed that I went along on several things I should have known better than to do."

"I imagine," he added, "permanent exile is punishment enough for this."

7. WHY WALL STREET IS BEING INVESTIGATED AGAIN

In the fall of 1961 Congress passed a resolution of both historic and contemporary importance. For the first time in nearly twenty-five years the nation's representatives ordered a full-scale probe of Wall Street.* The investigation, which is being conducted by a special staff of sixty-five Securities and Exchange Commission personnel, will examine almost every aspect of the Street's operations.† The main question it will attempt to answer is: how well is the public being protected in its securities dealings?

This concluding chapter will discuss why, after so many years of relative silence in relation to the Street, Congress saw fit to call for such a full scale probe. In doing so, this chapter will show some of the dramatic changes that have taken place in the securities' industry. It will examine too the latest fashion in manipulative techniques as well as some of the pitfalls into which the unsophisticated investor stumbles. Finally, this reporter will attempt to answer the ques-

* The 1955 stock market study of the Senate Banking and Currency Committee cannot be considered in this writer's opinion as searching as the current S.E.C. investigation.

† Congress has authorized an expenditure of $750,000 for the investigation.

tion: how well do Wall Street's and the Government's watchdogs protect the public?

The S.E.C.'s probe of the Street was in part triggered by
the exposure of the manipulations of Gerard A. Re his
son, Gerard F. Re, specialists on the American Stock Exchange. The Res—a facet of their activities was described in
detail in Chapter 4—had the distinction of managing the
most extensive rigging of the stock market since the late
1920's. Between 1954 and 1960 they illegally sold over one
million shares of nine corporations. The total value of these
securities came to more than ten million dollars. These manipulations, declared the S.E.C.'s Division of Trading and
Exchange, have resulted in "many millions of dollars of
harm to thousands of unsuspecting investors," and an estimated three million dollars in profits for the Res.

The Res, as specialists, stood at the very hub of the auction market. Not only were they privy to inside information,
but they were in a position to rig the market to their own
advantage. They did so with abandon and on occasion with a
sense of whimsy. Perhaps their wriest deal involved Rokeach
& Sons, a kosher foods manufacturer. The Res, who became
specialists for Rokeach, eventually gained control of the firm.
The elder Re helped Rokeach, the kosher foods maker, purchase Seamless Girdle Industries, a girdle company, from
Exquisite Form, a brassière manufacturer. With this wed-
ding of improbables accomplished, the Res proceeded illegally to unload their Rokeach stock. The net profit, lodged
in the dummy account of a former follower of Fulgencio Batista, came to more than $400,000. The Res, who dealt in
millions, had made it this time in salami.

Besides cheating the public, this father and son team even
managed to take advantage of their friends and acquaint-

ances. They were expert in spreading rumors and wined and dined brokers to whom they happily offered tips in the stocks they were manipulating. Among those to whom they touted stock were Toots Shor, the New York restaurateur; Chuck Dressen, manager of the Milwaukee Braves; Cookie Lavagetto, manager of the Minnesota Twins; Vincent F. Albano, Jr., Republican leader of New York's East Side; Abraham J. Gellinoff, chairman of the law committee of the New York County Democratic Party.

In its brief, the S.E.C.'s Division of Trading and Exchanges condemned the Res in the sharpest language. The brief concluded: "The securities laws arose from events which occurred over thirty years ago. Since that time and after the disclosure which resulted from both public and private investigation, the confidence of the public in the operation of the exchange markets has been slowly rebuilt. The Res, who, as specialists, stood at the very heart of an exchange market, have struck a heavy blow at that market."

On May 4, 1961, the Securities and Exchange Commission revoked the registration of the firm of Re, Re & Sagarese* and ordered the Res expulsion from the American Stock Exchange. The Res did not contest the facts as developed by the S.E.C.

Though the exposure of the Res' activities made dramatic headlines in the spring of 1961, the nation and the Street were to receive even more disturbing news. The next shock came with the sudden resignation of Edward Theodore Mc-Cormick in December, 1961, from the presidency of the American Stock Exchange. McCormick had risen from a $1,900 a year security analyst for the S.E.C. to a Commis-

---

* Robert J. Sagarese, a minor partner in the firm, was in no way implicated in the Res' activities.

sioner in 1949. Less than two years later he was elected president of the nation's second-largest auction market. When he resigned in December, 1961, he was earning $75,000 annually plus expenses. A Phi Beta Kappa and expert on the securities laws, he was the author of "Understanding the Securities Act and the S.E.C.," considered a standard work on the subject.

One reason for McCormick's sudden departure was the subsequent revelation of the following: In 1955 the then president of the American Stock Exchange had traveled to Miami and Havana where he was the guest of Alexander Guterma. McCormick later told the S.E.C. that he had incurred $5,000 in gambling debts which Guterma had paid. The financier at the time was attempting to obtain the listing of Shawano Development Corporation on the exchange (see Chapter 5). Shawano never achieved listing and McCormick, in allowing Guterma to pay his gambling debts, had not violated the law. Though the financier's activities had not been exposed at the time of McCormick's day at the gaming tables, the former S.E.C. Commissioner and stock exchange president had shown poor judgment to say the least.

McCormick's reign as president of the exchange illustrated a basic failing, the lack of adequate supervision and self-enforcement by the exchange of its own operations. This failing was publicly brought out in a shattering 127-page report issued by the S.E.C. on January 5, 1962. The report was a study of what had been occurring inside the American Stock Exchange during the past ten years.

The Commission's staff noted that McCormick was considered by the membership principally as a salesman rather than as an administrator, his main job being to solicit companies and obtain listing of their securities so that they would be traded on the exchange. The measure of his and the members' success in this endeavor may be briefly noted. Between 1951 and 1961 the number of companies with stocks listed rose from 763 to 1,000 and the volume of stocks traded from 110 million to 500 million. Just how busy Mc-Cormick kept himself in generating this additional business for the exchange was described in the S.E.C. report.

Members of the exchange's staff, the Federal agency said, reported new underwritings to McCormick, who in turn obtained a copy of the prospectus. He then phoned or wrote the company and asked it to apply for listing providing it seemed qualified. He also traveled throughout the country contacting officials of companies planning to issue stock. As the S.E.C. pointed out, McCormick had little time left to enforce the exchange's rules. And they sorely needed enforcing.

The Federal agency went on to note that the American Stock Exchange was in effect run by a chummy, tight-knit group of insiders consisting of three specialists and a former specialist. The specialists dominated the exchange government ment even though they represented only one of four classes of regular members.*

To understand the importance of the specialists' role and why the S.E.C. devoted nearly half of its report to their activities, it will be helpful to define their two main functions. One function is to serve as the broker's broker. In

---

* Of the 499 regular members of the American Stock Exchange, 160 are specialists. There are also 139 partners of member brokerage houses who execute buy and sell orders on the floor on behalf of their own houses, 140 two-dollar brokers who execute orders for member houses that do not have floor partners, and 60 floor traders who buy and sell for themselves with their own money.

this instance the specialist accepts orders from other brokers whose customers wish to buy or sell a stock at other than the current market price.

To illustrate, if you should wish to buy 100 shares of stock at $60 a share and the current market price is $65, your broker will leave your order with the specialist who has been assigned to that stock. The specialist then enters the order in his "book," the entry made after all the previous orders to buy the stock at $60. If the price of the stock should drop from $65 to $60 (the price at which you want to buy), then the specialist executes the requests to buy in the order in which he received them.

The second function of the specialist and the one that received the sharpest comments concerns the instances when the specialist buys and sells stock for his own profit and loss. By buying and selling from his own inventory of securities the specialist also helps to prevent erratic price fluctuations, or, to put it another way, maintain an orderly market in the stock.

For example, a stock has just sold at $28 a share. The lowest price any member of the public is willing to sell any-more of this stock is at $29 a share. The specialist, who maintains a personal inventory of this stock, offers to sell some of his shares at $28.25. This benefits the buyer who would obviously prefer to pay $28.25 instead of $29. It also allows for an orderly market or orderly rise or, as the case may be, decrease in price. (In the long run the specialist expects to make a profit out of these transactions.)

It is apparent that the specialist plays two roles, one that serves himself and the other that indirectly serves the public. These roles can come into conflict if the specialist is unethical or if there is not sufficient supervision on the part of an exchange. To put it another way, to maintain an orderly market, the specialist in his *public* role may be called upon to buy or sell at a loss for his own *private* account.* As a broker's broker he has the *public* function of collecting and knowing the general investors' secret buy and sell orders. Again he maintains the *private* function of buying and selling stock for himself.

According to the S.E.C., some specialists on the American Stock Exchange did the following:

1. Maintained close relations with the officers of companies in whose stock they specialized. They were thus able to gather information about the companies before it became public knowledge.

2. Bought shares of an issue before it was listed and then bought additional shares off the exchange for distribution on the exchange.

3. Showed their books to underwriters who planned distribution of large blocks of stock already outstanding. This gave the underwriters knowledge of the public demand for the stock.

4. Actively solicited new companies to have their stocks traded on the exchange. The specialists who were successful received as their reward the right to handle the stocks of these companies. (Following the exposure of the Res, the exchange instituted a ruling whereby new listings would be assigned "in the best interests of the exchange.")

These activities were allowed to exist because of inadequate supervision and enforcement on the part of the American Stock Exchange. This lax attitude was typified by the

---

* This can mean severe losses to some specialists. *The Wall Street Journal* records that one leading specialist's firm on the New York Stock Exchange lost $168,000 in its trading account in 1961.

following incident involving an unnamed specialist and James R. Dyer, a former chairman and one of the four men the S.E.C. said dominated the exchange.

Dyer, according to the Federal agency, testified that a specialist once told him when he was a floor governor that certain securities being offered on the exchange were in all probability part of a distribution of unregistered stock belonging to a control person. If so, this would be a clear violation of the Securities Act. Dyer, the S.E.C. said, told the specialist that his function was only to make a market in the security.

Dyer's reason for taking this attitude, the government agency declared, was that the brokerage firm offering the shares was an "old-line commission house," the type of firm "that wouldn't accept an order . . . unless it was proper." Then, without consulting counsel for the exchange or making any inquiry, Dyer told the specialist to execute the order without "interfering in somebody else's business."

In its overall conclusion, the S.E.C. declared:

"There can be little doubt that in the case of the American Stock Exchange the statutory scheme of self-regulation in the public interest has not worked out in the manner originally envisioned by Congress. The manifold and prolonged abuses by specialists and floor traders and other instances of misconduct described in this report make it clear that the problem goes beyond isolated violations and amounts to a general deficiency of standards and a fundamental failure of controls.

"Moreover, it is clear that the problem does not primarily consist of an absence or inadequacy of substantive rules of conduct. In certain respects the rules of the exchange are stronger than those of other exchanges and in recent months there has been a veritable flood of new provisions. Undoubtedly there are many areas where the substantive rules still require substantial improvement, but a mere proliferation of substantive rules will be useless if the people subject to the rules do not take them seriously and there are inadequate mechanisms for surveillance and enforcement."

The Federal agency added that it hoped the American Stock Exchange would correct its ways by itself. Then the S.E.C. warned, "The Commission must be prepared to exercise its supervisory powers if the necessary reform is not forthcoming."

It would appear at this writing that such reform is forthcoming. Several months prior to the release of the Federal agency's study, the exchange called for an independent, hard hitting investigation by Wall Street's own leaders. It was this investigation, incidentally, which turned up the information that led to McCormick's resignation. In fact, unknown to the Street's own investigative committee, the S.E.C. had been looking into the same allegations.*

Besides the conditions found in the American Stock Exchange, generated in part by its eager desire to expand, there exist other equally fundamental problems that the Street faces. It is these problems which explain Congress's call for the first major investigation of Wall Street in nearly a quarter of a century. To understand them, it would be helpful to describe some of the changes that have taken place in the Street itself during the past fifteen years.

Probably the most dramatic change that has occurred in the Street is the post-World War II rise in the number of

---

* Credit should be given to a journalistic beat by reporters Ed Cony and Lee Silberman of *The Wall Street Journal*. Three weeks before the information was officially released Cony and Silberman reported in the *Journal* the reasons behind McCormick's resignation.

small investors. As we entered 1962 there were more than fifteen million shareholders in the United States, more than double the number of a decade ago and ten times as many as in 1929. To put it another way, at least one out of eight adults today owns stocks, compared with one in sixteen in 1952. By 1970 it is expected the number of share owners may reach twenty-five million or more.

The arrival of a mass market for securities may be attributed to a number of factors: the rise in personal income and population, the growth of the nation's economy, the Street's campaign awakening people to the opportunities in becoming share owners, and the increase in the number and value of the securities themselves. There are now more than three thousand different securities that can be bought on the nation's exchanges. In addition the number of securities including municipal and government bonds available off the exchanges (over-the-counter) is estimated to exceed forty thousand. Finally, the outstanding value of all securities including government bonds and common stocks held by individuals came to nearly 445 billion dollars as we entered 1961. This is an increase of over 167 billion dollars in the past seven years. For the average investor there is little question that the judicial purchase of stocks and bonds can be a good way of making one's money grow.

Despite the advantages to the small investor, there does exist a danger in the mass marketing of an item as complex as securities. The danger is an appalling ignorance on the part of many small investors which makes them as an easy mark for highly speculative stocks and securities chicanery. A measure of the number of innocents abroad was suggested in a 1959 survey conducted by the New York Stock Exchange. According to the study, two out of five of the then current share owners were incapable of adequately defining a common stock.* Further, more than half of the estimated 12.8 million adults described as "on the threshold of investing" could not give an adequate definition. For the next group of 22.5 million who were interested in investing but had not considered it in the past year, three out of four could not answer the question: "What is a common stock?" Finally, nearly one-quarter of the last group viewed the chief advantage in buying common stock as the "opportunity for quick profit." It should also be noted that most shareowners and potential owners cannot afford substantial risks. Among the families of the 35.3 million potential securities buyers, a little more than half had annual incomes of under five thousand dollars.

The fairly widespread ignorance of many investors has been met in part through educational campaigns conducted by The New York Stock Exchange and several large brokerage houses. These efforts until recently had to overcome the post-World War II boom psychology that the market can only go up, and the gambling nature of many ordinary securities buyers. Typical of the concern shown were the two warnings issued by G. Keith Funston, president of the New York Stock Exchange. The warnings came about as a result of the speculative surge that gripped the market in the spring of 1961. After declaring on April 4 that "an overwhelming majority of investors" are using the marketplace

---

* Shareowners showed more intelligent motivation in buying common stocks than non-shareowners. Thus, 21 per cent of the shareowners offered "long term gain" as the advantage of purchasing common stock, followed by "good dividends" (19 per cent), "good when general prices go up" (17 per cent), "opportunity for quick profit" (14 per cent), "security for family, old age" (10 per cent), "automatic re-investment of dividends" (5 per cent), "other advantages" (14 per cent), "don't know" (6 per cent).

soundly, the head of the nation's largest exchange sounded this grim note:

"However, in some instances, there is disquieting evidence that some people have not yet discovered that it is impossible to get something for nothing, and they are attempting to make improper use of the facilities of the investment community. For example, reports reaching us indicate that some would-be investors are attempting to purchase shares of companies whose names they cannot identify, whose products are unknown to them, and whose prospects are, at best, highly uncertain."

The problem of the ignorant and sometimes hungry investor is compounded by still another factor, an increase in the activities of unscrupulous securities sellers, men of small conscience—a decided minority on the Street—who find the unsophisticated stock buyer an easy target.

This increase in fraudulent and unethical activities can be attributed in large measure to the dramatic rise in the Street's own business. Understandably, during the past boom decade there have been few growth industries that equal the increased business conducted by Wall Street itself. Between 1950 and 1961 the average daily volume of shares traded on the New York Stock Exchange rose from 1,980,000 to 4,000,000. The number of branch offices maintained by Big Board members has shown a 100 per cent increase. During the same ten-year period the number of customers' men (salesmen) registered with the National Association of Securities Dealers, the industry's over-the-counter policeman, has tripled. As a result of this rapid growth a number of these salesmen and brokers have had little previous experience or training in the field.

One salesman who has been selling securities for more

than ten years described what has happened. "Many people," he declared, "come into this business on a part time basis to supplement their incomes.* They find in most cases their extra income is greater than their earned income. So they quit their old jobs and become salesmen or brokers. One man I know who was a plumber's helper is now earning $50,000 a year as a securities salesman. Another man was earning $85 a week driving a cab. He now makes $500 a week selling mutual funds and stocks. Still another man, a cop, was selling securities on the side. Now he's given up moonlighting and is making $100,000 a year as a broker."

A consequence of this new element among a securities sales force that has reached more than one hundred and twenty thousand was described by William L. Cary, chairman of the Securities and Exchange Commission. Chairman Cary testified before the House subcommittee on Commerce and Finance. The Congressional subcommittee, headed by Representative Peter F. Mack, Jr. of Illinois, conducted a brief investigation of the securities markets in the spring of 1961. During his testimony Chairman Cary noted:

"Many securities salesmen work on a part-time basis; many have no particular qualifications to sell securities; and most important, many are not subject to the kind of supervision which insures high ethical standards. The possibility exists that these factors may have led to questionable merchandising techniques. They also have undermined the important personal relationship between broker and customer in which the broker seeks to ascertain whether the security is suitable for a particular customer."

The problem posed by the inadequately trained custom-

---

* Salesmen registered with the New York Stock Exchange must work full time in the securities business.

er's man is of extreme importance. Most investors, as has previously been shown, do not possess sufficient knowledge or information to be able to select by themselves those securities that would be appropriate to their needs. Thus, these investors, whose ignorance may only be matched by their gullibility, may find themselves in the perilous situation of having so poorly invested their funds that they lose their life savings.

It should be noted that the Street itself has been deeply concerned with this problem. Several brokerage houses have at times refused to handle cheap, risky securities. In addition, both the New York Stock Exchange and the National Association of Securities Dealers have markedly stiffened their examinations which salesmen must pass to become registered representatives. Under the old N.A.S.D. examination, for example, the prospective customer's man received a booklet that contained the questions and answers that would be used in the exam. Thus, all the salesmen had to do was memorize the booklet. A boob could pass and undoubtedly some did. Under the new N.A.S.D. exam, which became effective at the start of 1962, passing is not only tougher but the salesman has to know much more.* For one, the new test is multiple choice, not true and false as in the old examination. But even more important, the salesman is given a suggested list of books to study, but does not see any of the questions and answers beforehand. Finally, the subjects under the new exam cover the entire securities market as well

---

* The difference between the old and new N.A.S.D. tests may be seen in the following figures. In 1961 the old exam was taken by 30,790 people with only 3 per cent failing. In January, 1962, the first month of the new test, 10 per cent failed. Interestingly, in December, 1961, the last month the old and easier exam was offered, 6,078 took it. In the following month when the new and harder test was given, only 557 would-be-brokers tried it.

as the N.A.S.D. rules of fair play. However, there still remain some twenty-five thousand securities salesmen who do not come under the jurisdiction of any exchange or the N.A.S.D. and may not have taken any examination, including those given by some states.†

Still another problem the Street faces is the get-rich-quick psychology that accompanied the post-World War II boom market. This attitude feeds on rising prices, rumors and tips which may be generated by such unseasoned experts as housewives, taxicab drivers and barbers. A story, though apocryphal, illustrates the ease with which some individuals risk their savings on securities they know nothing about.

As the tale goes, a man recently received a stock tip from his barber who was boosting a company called Ultrasonics Precision. The customer gave the tip to his broker and told him to purchase four hundred shares. Two weeks later he went for another haircut. During the conversation the barber said he had been misunderstood and had actually recommended a different company, Ultrasonics Industries, not Ultrasonics Precision. The customer called his broker again and ordered him to make the change. The broker did and the man made an eight hundred dollar profit on the sale of the "wrong" stock.

The moral to this story, if there be one, is that in some instances even fools make money. Actually, on the long count, they usually lose it. However, the attitude of uninformed speculation persists and has helped give rise to one of the major problems on the Street—the so-called hot issues.

A hot issue is simply the flotation of new stock which over-

† At least thirty-five states license securities salesmen and thirteen of these states use tests in the licensing process.

night or longer may increase as much as one hundred per cent above the initial offering price. The new issues, all of which are sold off the exchanges (over-the-counter), are frequently highly speculative offerings of new companies making their first stock sales to the public. It should be emphasized at this point that there is nothing basically wrong with this method of raising money for small young companies. It is one of the ways new industry can grow. Also a hot issue may not necessarily mean that the stock's sudden rise in price is unwarranted. The company's prospects and legitimate public demand may prove valid reasons for the increase. Nevertheless, speculation in new issues has caused concern and alarm in Wall Street. This concern was expressed again by Funston on May 16, 1961, in his second warning within six weeks. The New York Stock Exchange president declared, in part:

"There still seems to be a preoccupation with 'low-priced' shares because they are low-priced; and an unhealthy appetite for 'new issues' of unseasoned companies merely because they are new. As experienced investors have long known, neither 'low-price' nor 'new issues' are guarantees of anything—except, perhaps, a proportionately greater degree of risk.

"It is clear that in these areas some people are feverishly substituting rumor, hearsay and a desire to get rich quick for sound investment judgment. Some new offerings, for example, are greeted clamorously by those who tell their brokers, in effect: 'Don't bother me with the facts, get me some of that stock!'

"Such concentration in low-priced shares and 'new issues' makes a mockery of the word 'investing.'"

There are a number of reasons why new issues are so vulnerable to speculation. They are frequently low-priced and thus easily fit within the bank account of the average investor. Secondly, many new issues have what the Street happily calls a "small float." This means that only a few shares are available which, if a demand exists, automatically raises the price. The reason for the shortage is that many new issues consist of stocks being sold by a company for the first time. Since no others are on the market, the supply is naturally limited. Not only the customer but also the salesman must be continually alert if he expects to obtain shares of a new issue that is in short supply. One salesman told me he had missed his allotment by taking a few minutes off from his desk and going to the washroom. He added that he discovered upon returning that all he would have received was five shares.

The third reason for the popularity of new issues is that many represent the latest fad in glamour stocks like uranium, electronics, bowling, cosmetics, teaching machines and publishing, to name a few. At one time or another they have held the promise of elephantine growth. Some investors, I might add, do not limit their selections to the latest securities with sex appeal. The top financial executive of one of the nation's biggest corporations has continuously bid for almost every new issue that has come on the market.

Perhaps most disturbing are that the factors which have made new issues so attractive to wild speculation have also made them particularly suited to outright manipulation. According to a number of people I have talked to on the Street, manipulations in new issues occur frequently and with regularity, particularly during boom times. Furthermore, these manipulations are often impossible to detect. Though there are many variations used, the manipulative techniques follow a classic pattern. A trader for an over-the-counter house explained what may happen.

"No new issue will get off the ground unless people want it," he said. "To create the demand the salesmen for the selling group start touting the stock to their customers. The original underwriting was one hundred thousand shares with an offering price at three dollars a share. The salesmen, who have been telling their customers what a great potential the company has, actually have oversold the issue. In other words, they have customers for one hundred and fifty thousand shares, though only one hundred thousand actually exist. Obviously they can't deliver all these shares. So a demand has already been created.

"The salesmen, however, do not stop there. They use a device called tie-in sales. In this case they tell the customer he can have one thousand shares at the initial offering price of three dollars providing he agrees to purchase another thousand shares at four and one-half dollars in the after-market [after the stock is on the market and being traded]. Meanwhile, the underwriter or the other houses in the selling group have given a number of shares to insiders—favored customers and other brokers—who promise to hold the stock and not sell it until they are told." [This practice by the underwriter or broker is known as free-riding and withholding, and has been banned by the N.A.S.D.]

Thus an artificial demand is created for the stock. At the same time, the number of shares available for trading is already in short supply. Following the natural laws of commercial gravity, when the demand is greater than the supply prices go in only one direction—up. For the underwriters, brokers and favored customers—usually people who buy often and heavily—these manipulations can mean handsome profits. For the general public which does not receive favored treatment and invests in a Wall Street sweepstake it may mean they lose their investment if they hold their stock too long.

According to Philip A. Loomis, Jr., director of the S.E.C.'s Division of Trading and Exchanges in Washington, hot issues that have been manipulated are extremely difficult to detect. In the first place, not all hot issues are the result of manipulations. Secondly, some of the techniques used in a manipulation such as overselling an issue and giving stock to preferred customers are common practices on the Street and are not in themselves illegal or unethical. What may make them illegal is the underwriter's and selling group's intent, a hard point to prove. Tie-in sales, of course, are illegal, but they too are difficult to detect.

"The S.E.C.," Loomis said, "simply does not have the manpower or the time to check all hot issues. All we can do is spot-check them. But it is difficult to get anywhere. First we go to the underwriter and get the names of the selling group. Then we get the names of the traders and the public who bought the stock. We run into thousands of names. Then we start talking to people. We find a lot of people out to lunch. And when we do talk to them they do not tell you anything. Unless a hot issue has cooled, the investors are happy."

The National Association of Securities Dealers, the self-regulating organization of the over-the-counter market, has also tried valiantly to deal with the problem. The increasing importance that hot issues have played in N.A.S.D. investigations was brought out in testimony before the Mack subcommittee.

In 1956 the association had sent out 817 questionnaires to underwriters and selling groups of three hot issues. During the first nine months of 1961 some 3,191 questionnaires were sent out covering sixty-six hot issues. The purpose of these questionnaires was to learn whether the underwriters and selling groups had violated N.A.S.D. rules in bringing out the securities offerings.

Though the questionnaires may appear self-serving—what results can you expect if you ask a man whether he is breaking the rules—the N.A.S.D. points out that false answers, if discovered, can lead to expulsion. The association also periodically investigates all its members. Despite these efforts the N.A.S.D. at this writing has yet to prove manipulation in any hot issue. However, it has found violations of its free-riding and withholding regulation, which can be a manipulative device. The difficulty in proving manipulation of hot issues was shown again in testimony before the House subcommittee headed by Representative Mack.

MACK: There would be no question, though, about artificial stimulation being a manipulation of a stock?

MARC A. WHITE [N.A.S.D. Counsel]: Do you mean artificial stimulation at the time of the offering or thereafter?

MACK: I would presume at the time of the offering.

WHITE: Certainly if we could prove that, we would take action on it, if not under the interpretation, then under the rules of fair practice.

MACK: At the same time, do you investigate tie-in sales, or is that more difficult to investigate?

WILLIAM H. CLAFLIN III [then N.A.S.D. Board Chairman]: Usually you have to be tipped on tie-in sales. In other words, you have to have somebody who tells you that it is tied in. So it is apt to come in from a complaint from a member of the public. But just going in and looking at the records, unless you have been warned, you would have quite a bit of difficulty picking it up in a routine examination. It is a hard thing to catch someone at.

MACK: What has been your experience with the tie-in sales? Have you had quite a few complaints or tips concerning the tie-in sales which you have investigated?

CLAFLIN: Actually, I don't know that we have a case on that.

WHITE: We have no case on it. My knowledge of it stems from conversations or the newspapers. By that I don't mean that it probably doesn't exist, but I have no personal knowledge of it.

MACK: The people in the industry generally are acquainted with the procedure involved, and it seems to be a practice in the industry, but I conclude that your investigations haven't been successful in proving a case.

WHITE: In that particular area, we do not have a case as yet.

The inherent difficulties in detecting manipulations that may occur in a hot issue illuminate a more basic problem, policing the over-the-counter market itself, undoubtedly the most complex area of enforcement in the securities industry. To understand why this is so, it would be helpful to describe briefly how the over-the-counter market differs from trading on the exchanges.

Actually, the term over-the-counter is a misnomer, for no trading is done over a counter. In contrast to the exchanges like the Big Board and the American Stock Exchange, there is no central place where securities are bought and sold. Instead, on the over-the-counter market stocks and bonds are traded through thousands of individual brokerage houses throughout the country!

A second difference of utmost importance is that prices of the securities traded over-the-counter are arrived at through negotiation. Thus, the customer by shopping around (or by having his brokerage house do it for him) may encounter a variety of prices for the particular stock at any moment during the day. In contrast, the stock exchanges are auction markets. Thus when a security is purchased on the New York Stock Exchange, for example, the buyer, the moment his purchase is made, could not go somewhere else on the same exchange and get a different price. Of course, in both the over-the-counter market and the exchanges the prices paid for securities may vary throughout the day.

The over-the-counter market is different from an exchange in still another fashion. It is larger in almost every way. Five times as many securities are regularly traded over-the-counter as on the New York Stock Exchange. The total daily dollar volume probably exceeds that of all the exchanges combined. In fact, in sheer size the over-the-counter market cannot be compared with any other securities market in the United States. It also is unique in the variety of the quality of the securities that are traded, ranging from U. S. Government bonds, bank and insurance stocks, to low-priced, highly speculative issues. It is the place where new, unseasoned companies start out, some eventually moving into the more rarefied atmosphere of an exchange. It is also the place where big companies like Ford and American Tel and Tel sell additional securities. Thus, it is the home of some of the safest securities in the world and some of the worst "cats and dogs."

The changes that have taken place in the over-the-counter market are as dramatic as any of those in the Street. Of all the divisions of the securities industry, few can compare with the over-the-counter's growth. This development can be illustrated by the increase in membership of the National

Association of Securities Dealers, made up of those who deal in stocks traded off the exchanges. (Practically all exchange member firms, except exchange specialists, are also members of the N.A.S.D.) Here are just a few startling figures. In 1946 the association had 2,514 member firms. As of May 30, 1961, the number of firms had climbed to 4,586, more than double. Within the same period the number of the member firms's branch offices had increased five-fold and the number of salesmen had grown from some twenty-three thousand to over ninety-three thousand.

All these facts and figures point up the amorphous nature of the over-the-counter market, which, vast in size, stretches to probably every major city in the country. Much of the policing of this market is carried out by the National Association of Securities Dealers and its members.

The N.A.S.D. came into being on August 7, 1939, as the result of passage of the Maloney Amendment to the Securities and Exchange Act of 1934. Senator Francis T. Maloney of Connecticut who introduced the legislation explained why the N.A.S.D. was formed. He declared:

". . . there can be no large group of people engaged in any industry enjoying potentialities for profit, which does not attract the careless or the greedy few who bring discredit upon the entire group unless prevented by regulation from so doing. It is with this problem of imposing proper standards of business conduct upon that small minority . . . that we have all been wrestling for years.

"The machinery of [the securities] business is delicate. It can be dislocated either by corruption from within or by unwise and burdensome regulation from without. Our task is to prevent the former without risk of the latter. The [Maloney] Act provides a formula designed to accomplish this result. This formula is predicated upon the principle that corruption from within, so far as possible, should be prevented from *within* and that external restraints should be rendered unnecessary as a result of the exercise of self-restraint."

The difficult task of regulating a free market is accomplished through the N.A.S.D.'s headquarters in Washington and thirteen district offices located throughout the United States. The association's members are required to live by a thick book of rules which may be summed up by the N.A.S.D. creed: "A member, in the conduct of his business, shall observe high standards of commercial honor and just and equitable principles of trade." The rules and the creed are strictly enforced. A staff of more than thirty investigators make surprise examinations of all members at least once every three years. If a member firm bears closer scrutiny, examinations are made more frequently.

If it appears that any violations have occurred, the complaint, which also may be registered by the public or another member, is filed with one of thirteen District Business Conduct Committees, made up of fellow securities brokers and others in the industry who are members of the N.A.S.D. The members of these committees serve without pay. They apparently feel service is both an honor and a duty.

Hearings are held and the man against whom a complaint has been lodged may attend with counsel. If he is found guilty he may appeal the decision to the N.A.S.D.'s Board of Governors. If the Governors turn down his plea, he then may appeal to the Securities and Exchange Commission, and if that fails, he may seek relief in a Federal court. All N.A.S.D. decisions are automatically referred to the S.E.C.

which also may take action if the violations fall within the Commission's jurisdiction.

Though the N.A.S.D., like the S.E.C., cannot send a man to jail—that is up to the Justice Department and the Federal Courts—the Association does have the power to censure, fine, suspend or expel a member and his registered representatives. Why the power to suspend and expel proves effective can be explained by the following:

Members in dealing with one another receive concessions on the same basis that wholesalers do when they trade. However, a non-member dealing with a N.A.S.D. member pays a retail price like the public, which means he will make little if any profit. Since nearly all over-the-counter firms are members of the association, this penalty serves as a severe economic sanction.*

Despite the safeguards offered in the Maloney Amendment and the earnest endeavors of the N.A.S.D., the vast, amorphous over-the-counter market poses special enforcement problems which have yet to be solved. One of the more obvious problems is the variety of prices that may be quoted at any one time in the sale of a security. Furthermore, unlike a trade on an exchange where the current quote is flashed throughout the country only moments after a transaction, prices of securities traded over-the-counter are not published until the close of the trading day. The National Quota-

---

* Under the Maloney Amendment membership in the N.A.S.D. is open to all brokers and dealers authorized to transact any branch of the investment banking and securities business in the United States subject to certain exceptions. These include prior expulsion from a registered stock exchange or the N.A.S.D., revocation of registration by the S.E.C., and conviction of a felony or misdemeanor in the past ten years involving embezzlement, fraudulent conversion, misappropriation of funds or abuse or misuse of a fiduciary relationship.

tion Bureau, which daily gathers and publishes the *wholesale* price ranges (the price the broker pays) for more than 7,500 securities, puts its lists in the hands of subscribing brokers no later than nine the following morning. The N.A.S.D. collects regularly the *retail* price ranges (the price the public pays) for more than 3,000 securities each day, almost as many securities as are available on all the nation's exchanges. These quotations are then sent to newspapers throughout the country, where they are published that evening or the following morning. According to Wallace H. Fulton, the N.A.S.D.'s executive director, on January 2, 1962, the association started making retail quotations available to New York newspapers twice each day, a chore of no simple proportions.

The problem of spotting chicanery is further complicated in the over-the-counter market by the almost total absence of information available on the number of shares traded. As Commissioner Cary of the S.E.C. noted in his testimony before the Mack subcommittee, "For example, unlike the exchange markets, the volume of trading is not known. Thus, it is difficult to determine which securities are active and which inactive or whether price increases or decreases in a security have been accompanied by slight or heavy trading."

Thus, a violent change in prices and volume—the two automatic signals that show a manipulation may be occurring —are not immediately apparent on the over-the-counter market. This means in effect that the N.A.S.D., the S.E.C., and the public may not know for hours when a sudden and spectacular rise or decrease in prices has taken place. Equally important, both enforcement organizations and the public have no way of knowing whether there has been a marked increase or decrease in the number of shares sold over-the-counter, the second signal that may show chicanery has occurred.

It should be noted that both the S.E.C. and the N.A.S.D. are aware of these drawbacks in the day-to-day policing of the over-the-counter trading. Avery Rockefeller, Jr., the current chairman of the N.A.S.D., reports that his association has begun setting up a stock clearing corporation which, among other services, will report the volume of securities traded over-the-counter. This experiment, the first of its kind for the over-the-counter market, is taking place in New York, where a large portion of the trading occurs.

In addition several electronic systems have been installed in brokerage houses that report representative sales of some over-the-counter securities. One system, for example, makes it possible for price ranges to be obtained every fifteen minutes during the day. However, it will probably take at least several years before the stock clearing corporation and the electronic price reporting systems are sufficiently refined and widely enough employed by the industry to give a total and immediate picture of daily over-the-counter trading.

There is still another area where basic information is frequently lacking. This involves the monthly, semiannual and annual financial reports which must be filed by companies listed on an exchange, but which are not required of many firms whose securities are traded exclusively off the exchanges. This significant and vital difference between the over-the-counter market and the exchanges was summed up by Chairman Cary in this testimony before the Mack subcommittee.

"A large but unknown number of issuers, in whose securities there is a substantial public interest," declared Chairman Cary, "are not subject to these reporting requirements. Thus, the investing public is deprived of financial information with respect to these companies, a void emphasized by the fact that many of them do not even appear in the standard financial reference works. This absence of data is particularly unfortunate in the over-the-counter market area, where a great number of companies are speculative or unseasoned ventures. In summary, we note this gap in the full disclosure requirements of the securities laws and state our view that any investigation should concern itself with the fundamental problem of the over-the-counter market."

In contrast to the over-the-counter market, those who police the exchanges have readily at their command the type of trading information previously mentioned. In addition they possess the obvious advantage of having all the transactions occur in one central location, the floor of the exchanges themselves. Thus, if any danger signals should flare, the exchanges' watchdogs can immediately step in and temporarily halt trading or call for an on-the-spot investigation.

The two most important stock exchanges are the Big Board or New York Stock Exchange and the American Stock Exchange. Of the 36.7 billion dollars worth of securities traded on twelve registered exchanges during the first half of 1961, 30.1 billion could be accounted for on the Big Board and 4.3 billion on the American. Of the remaining 2.3 billion volume, 1.5 billion was attributed to the Midwest and Pacific Coast exchanges. Eight other exchanges accounted for the rest.*

---

* These include the following exchanges: Boston, Cincinnati, Detroit, Philadelphia-Baltimore, Pittsburgh, Salt Lake, San Francisco Mining and Spokane. The Chicago Board of Trade, an exchange also registered with the S.E.C., showed no securities traded and the new National Stock Exchange had not yet begun to operate. There are also four exempted exchanges. It should

Certainly the most important stock exchange and the center of the nation's auction market is the Big Board. The exchange, founded in 1792, has grown from a membership of twenty-four men to 1,366. Originally located under a buttonwood tree, the Big Board now disgorges forth such impressive statistics as a trading room five stories high, forty miles of pneumatic tubing laced under the floor and 1,300 private telephone lines directly connecting the floor of the exchange with member firm offices. All these mechanical facilities serve as a series of funnels through which the public's buy and sell orders (a daily average of 60,000 in 1961) are handled. It is this frenetic activity originating from London and Paris to San Francisco and Hartford that makes the Big Board the nation's biggest auction market and a police operation of sizable proportions.

Like the N.A.S.D., the New York Stock Exchange is policed by its own members and personnel. This supervision covers three important areas: the day-to-day trading, the activities of member firms, and the companies whose securities are listed on the exchange.

The daily trading operation receives the most immediate scrutiny. Thirty members of the exchange are on the floor each day. They constantly watch, among other things, the tape which is in full view and gives almost instantaneously the price paid and the number of shares involved in each sale. They observe too the nineteen posts where the exchange's 1,350 issues may be traded.

They also watch over the specialist, the broker's broker

---

be noted that the exchanges outside New York also trade in a number of securities listed on the leading New York exchanges. These are known as dual listings and are given unlisted trading privileges on the out-of-town exchanges.

whose main job is to maintain a fair and orderly market. (How well the Big Board's specialists do their job in maintaining an orderly market is illustrated by the fact that about 85 per cent of their trades involved buying when everyone else was selling and selling when others were buying.) These men, whose operations form the heart of the auction market, number 350 on the New York Stock Exchange.

If during the day there should be a marked variation in price and volume—observable either from the tape or the trading on the floor itself—a member of the exchange's floor committee may halt trading temporarily while an investigation is conducted. At the end of the day the specialist files a report on all his trading activities. He is also checked at least four times a year by surprise audits of his books.

A significant part of the on-the-scene watchdog activities of the exchange's floor officials is the Big Board's stock watching department. This group uses an I.B.M. computer, among other tools, to spot unusual price movements and volume changes. It then investigates the reasons behind the apparent abnormal activity.

The second area of surveillance involves the Big Board's brokerage houses which make up the majority of firms that belong to the exchange. Like the N.A.S.D., the New York Stock Exchange maintains its own group of examiners specially trained to spot violations of the exchange's rules and regulations. Their examinations of the firms' books occur at least once a year. In addition, three other surprise audits are held each year of each member's records. As in the case of the N.A.S.D., the Big Board may fine, suspend or expel a member if a violation is found and the penalty is warranted. The economic sanction of expulsion again is sufficient to drive the violator out of the securities business.

The final control exercised by the exchange consists of the Big Board's power to delist the securities which it admits for trading. Thus, for a company to be allowed to have its securities traded on the exchange it must maintain these minimum qualifications: one-half million common shares outstanding whose total market value is at least ten million dollars plus three hundred stockholders, each of whose holdings consist of at least one hundred shares. Virtually all of these companies are called upon by the exchange to file financial reports once every three months. No other exchange, incidentally, can make that statement. (As in the case of Guterma and F. L. Jacobs, failure to file the required financial data led to suspension of the companies' securities.)

Though the American Stock Exchange is nowhere as old, large or sedate as the New York Stock Exchange, it is striving to compete with the Big Board where it can. The American Stock Exchange is smaller in many ways. It has half the number of listed securities, less than half the number of specialists and its floor trading area is half the size of a football field compared to the Big Board's which runs the full hundred yards. However, despite these differences the American offers what the Big Board does not, a seasoning ground for new companies. A little more than 41 per cent of the securities traded on the Big Board got their start on the smaller exchange. Though these issues are no longer traded on the American, a number of sizable, older companies who could qualify for the Big Board have remained with the smaller exchange. The American is also quick to point out that 88 per cent of its members also belong to the New York Stock Exchange.

In policing their activities, however, both exchanges have

generally similar rules and enforcement procedures. The differences, where they exist, have more to do with size. The American Stock Exchange, for example, has semiannual reporting procedures of companies with listed securities while the Big Board requires quarterly reports. The American Stock Exchange also had 195 companies whose securities were unlisted* compared to the older exchange where there are none. Though companies with unlisted securities are not required by law to issue financial reports, the American Exchange says such information is obtained and made available in its public reading room.†

As noted earlier, following the Re and Re debacle the American has made substantial improvements in its rules governing the activities of its specialists. It also plans some crucial reforms as the result of an exhaustive investigation conducted by a special exchange appointed committee.‡ In addition the smaller exchange will have operating by 1963 a three-million-dollar electronic computer which will supply more instantaneous information to the public than the Big Board gives. At the same time the computer should materially improve the American's stock watching operations. It should be noted that computers, though handy tools, do not remove the need for human experts to recognize a manipulative pattern and officials to act quickly and forcefully when such violations occur.

* As of September 25, 1961.
† See Chapter 4 for the manipulation of Swan-Finch, an unlisted security.
‡ This nine-member committee, appointed in October, 1961, was headed by Gustave L. Levy, a partner of Goldman Sachs & Co. The committee consisted mainly of large Wall Street brokerage firms. Among the Levy group's proposals was a call for strengthening the exchange presidency through added powers and a bigger staff. It would also limit the governing board's duties to policy making. In addition, it would broaden the board's representation to include member firms outside the New York City area.

Finally, we come to the master watchdog, the Securities and Exchange Commission, which simultaneously complements and supersedes Wall Street's own self-regulations. As noted in Chapter 1, the exchanges, like the N.A.S.D., must register with the Commission. In so doing they must show they are organized in such a way that they can comply with the Securities Acts and provide for fair dealing and protection of investors. Indicative of the Commission's power is the little known provision of the 1934 Act which permits the S.E.C. with the approval of the President to close down any national exchange for ninety days if in the Commission's opinion such action is deemed necessary in the public interest.

The Commission's powers extend beyond the exchanges and the N.A.S.D. and include surprise inspections of 5,200 brokers and dealers throughout the United States who also must register with the S.E.C. If the S.E.C. discovers that a broker-dealer has violated the law or its own regulations, the Commission may revoke his registration or suspend him and his firm from membership in an exchange or the N.A.S.D.* As mentioned previously under the full disclosure principle, the S.E.C. is also responsible for examinations of new issues that seek registration with the Commission, proxy solicitations and insider trading reports.

These functions and many others are carried out by a relatively small, highly trained staff of nearly 1,000 attorneys, security analysts and examiners, investigators, engineers, as well as administrative and clerical employees. The five commissioners and two out of three members of the staff are located in the S.E.C.'s Washington headquarters. The re-

* See Chapter 3 for how the S.E.C. employed its broker-dealer inspections to close down boiler rooms financed in part by the underworld.

mainder are scattered throughout nine regional and eight branch offices. It is the regional offices which serve as the precincts where the patrolmen watch over the day-to-day operations of Wall Street. The center of the S.E.C.'s market-surveillance department naturally enough is located at the Regional Office in New York. The man there in charge of the minute-by-minute check on the market is Frederic M. Curran.

Tall, imposing, with a mind that clicks along like a Recordak unreeling microfilm, Curran has two loves—the Navy and the Street—both of which have given him absorbing careers. As a Naval officer his experiences were unusual. During World War I he became an ensign, though only seventeen at the time. He said he was twenty-one. During the next World War Curran served as the commanding officer of the *U.S.S. Jamestown,* then the world's largest yacht that boasted such luxuries as soap dishes and shower-curtain rings made out of 18-karat gold. Originally owned by the Cadwalladers of Philadelphia and the Roeblings who built the Brooklyn Bridge, the *Jamestown* had been turned into a tender for PT boats. After a considerable stint of sailing around the North Atlantic in another ship, Curran was transferred to the War College at Newport, Rhode Island, and then to the head of the combat intelligence staff of Fleet Admiral King. He emerged from the Navy in 1946 as a captain.

Though nautical terms occasionally slip into his speech, Curran has little time these days to think about boats or the sea. His big job is to keep watch on some ten thousand different securities that are traded daily on the nation's various securities markets. His knowledge of the market and the chicanery that can take place is the result of nearly forty years of experience. As a matter of fact, his very first job was working for one of Wall Street's most accomplished swindlers.

"I started learning early," he recalls. "I was a call boy in a large investment house. This meant that I served as the personal messenger of one of the firm's prized accounts. As it turned out the 'lone wolf' I worked for was Ivar Kreuger."

One of the first meetings Curran attended was a talk on the proposed underwriting for Swedish Match, one of Kreuger's lucrative ventures. "I remember the speaker holding up a book of matches. 'If five of these matchsticks are duds,' the speaker declared, 'profit for Swedish Match goes up five per cent. If ten are duds, profits go up fifteen per cent.'"

By 1934, Curran had further broadened his experience, serving as a trader, customer's man and eventually a partner in a brokerage house. He was then about thirty-five. It was at this point that Curran decided to become a government man. Congress had passed the Securities and Exchange Act setting up the S.E.C. and Joseph Kennedy had become the Commission's first chairman. Curran called on the elder Kennedy, spending twenty minutes selling himself. When he walked out, Curran took with him an appointment as one of five trading inspectors. Except for six years in the Navy during World War II, Curran has spent the intervening years with the S.E.C.

Fred Curran's working day actually begins the previous night when he sits down in his home to read the latest periodicals describing world, national and business events. During the evening hours he will be busy digesting the *London Economist,* the *Manchester Guardian, Fortune, Business Week,* reports from the American Institute of Economic Research, as well as concentrating on his own private studies.

By the time he has arrived at the S.E.C.'s office in downtown New York, Curran will have absorbed *The New York Times,* the *New York Herald Tribune* and *The Wall Street Journal.*

For the next two hours, the head of market surveillance reads his mail, which consists of three hundred pieces each week. It includes sixty brokers' stock market letters, Federal Reserve monthly reviews, S.E.C. statistical bulletins, Moody's, Standard and Poor's, trading reports on the Canadian exchanges, to name a few. All this background material may serve either to reinforce what Curran already knows and has predicted or give him leads for securities that may need special watching.

Once he has finished his mail he begins checking the "pink sheets" which one day not so long ago contained over 200 legal-size pages that carried 8,000 individual stock issues inserted by 2,000 over-the-counter brokers. He also checks through the daily and weekly trading sheets of ten out-of-town stock exchanges. The real working day has yet to begin. It starts promptly at 10 A.M. when the Big Board and American tapes begin to record the tens of thousands of transactions that will occur during that day's trading. At this point two analyst tape watchers take up their posts for a continuous trade-by-trade surveillance of the two exchanges. Together they log all changes in the prices of about 250 stocks including those that are most active as well as the securities considered "suspect." Curran, who oversees this operation, is also busy answering phones—an inquiry from the staff or a tip of a forthcoming manipulation or violation which he may receive from one of hundreds of "contacts" on the Street. But for Frederic Curran the great skill is the ability to read the series of quotations that emerge on the

Big Board and American tapes and to know what they mean.

"For some people," he said, "the tape is just a series of hieroglyphics and numbers. For me watching the tape is like reading the chapters of a novel with more of the plot evolving each day."

What Curran and his analysts look for are patterns of wrongdoing that may be signaled by price and volume variations. Sometimes only the barest hint of activity can arouse Curran's curiosity. "Suppose a stock has been quiescent. Then the tape begins recording the purchase of a couple of hundred shares each day. The price of the stock is not even being raised. But what may be happening is someone is accumulating stock right under your eyes. Somebody is under the apple tree waiting for the apple to drop. He doesn't shake the tree. In fact, he doesn't even want you to know he is in the orchard."

If this or any other activity seems unusual Curran has it checked out. Much of this activity is quickly explained after an examination of the Dow Jones ticker which carries both business and non-business news. Thus, a split, a merger, dividend announcement or general news development can justify a stock's sharp movement. Curran also has at his command an intelligence file that covers some four thousand securities. This file contains the latest information that in any way could affect a stock's activity. If no acceptable explanation is forthcoming, the security in question is then placed on the surveillance department's special watch list where its movement is logged for the next four to five days. If the security's erratic behavior continues, Curran will write a memo suggesting an investigation or quiz.

It is at this point that one of the Regional Office's investigators may be ordered into action. If the stock under scrutiny is traded on an exchange, he will contact the security's specialist who keeps a record of all the brokers who have placed buy and sell orders for the stock under suspicion. In an emergency a detail of investigators may be sent to the exchange and the specialist will be called off the floor. Once the information from the specialist has been gathered, the investigator either sends out questionnaires or calls the individual brokers. The brokers, in turn, supply him with the date on which the transaction takes place, the day when the broker receives or delivers the shares, the number of shares involved, the price, and the name of the account the broker was serving. The account may be listed in the name of another broker, bank or other organization. To find the actual customer will mean additional leg work and checking.

While the above information has been flowing in from the brokers, the investigator is kept busy searching for an essential item, the exact time the transactions took place. For example, he may discover that most sell orders occurred during the day with heavy buying only at the very end of that day's trading. This may mean that someone has been attempting to unload a large block of securities without lowering the market price. The investigator will obtain the time element of a security traded on the New York Stock Exchange by checking the Fitch sheets which give the day's trading in chronological order and the odd-lot dealers (those who trade in odd-lots of less than one hundred shares) who must keep an account of the time of their transactions. (The American Exchange itself supplies time, volume and price.)

With this information at his command, the investigator then fills in a chart which shows when a customer bought stock, the person who sold it, the price paid, the quote on the market before the stock was sold, the new price, and the number of shares involved. The investigator can then tell whether the customer's purchase resulted in an increase in price or, if a seller, a decrease. He can also spot whether the buying or selling is originating from one geographic area like Kalamazoo or New York, whether one individual is operating through a group of brokers, whether a number of unrelated people are involved, and finally whether one or many brokerage houses are doing the buying or selling.

The investigator, as a result of all this effort, has reconstructed the entire day's, week's or month's transactions in a particular security. There have been occasions when an investigator has been able to reconstruct a market involving one million shares which have been bought and sold through three hundred brokers for five thousand accounts scattered throughout the world. To put it another way, if a major manipulation has taken place an S.E.C. investigator will probably do more leg work and will have to fit together more pieces of a puzzle than any other type of criminal investigator. For the whole to be meaningful, the man from the S.E.C. must not only possess years of experience in the Street but an exact knowledge of how the market operates.

As one investigator put it, "There is a chink in every piece of armor. Once you have found the chink everything falls into place. In the case of a manipulation, this chink or weakness which may have been overlooked by the perpetrators can be discovered in many ways. This includes not only the investigative work just mentioned but sworn testimony, confidential sources, intuitiveness on the investigator's part. There is no avenue of investigation that is considered so small that it is not checked."

The main reason the S.E.C. prober's job has become so complicated is that the modern manipulation is more complex and devious. In the old days before Congress passed the Securities Acts and created the Commission, the manipulator would not go to such extremes to hide his identity. "To-day," continued the S.E.C. investigator, "the manipulator may induce others to purchase the stock, giving them a cash bonus and guaranteeing them against loss. He will employ dummy accounts that may be located in foreign countries, banks or brokerage firms, over which the S.E.C. has no jurisdiction."

In summary it may be said with certainty that while the securities manipulations and frauds of today are often subtler and more difficult to detect, they do not compare in scope with those of the lawless years. Furthermore, the public has the protection of the Federal Government, the Securities Acts, and Wall Street itself, which earnestly endeavors to root out the thief and the scoundrel. As noted earlier, men like Tellier, Birrell and Guterma may have fooled both the Street and the public, but they do not represent the financial community. They are the pirates who raid wantonly and without scruple. It should be expected that other buccaneers with similar talents will try to succeed where they failed. Undoubtedly there will be other cases too of men like the Res who are of the Street, but who betray the trust the Street has given them. It is an obvious axiom that no law, penalty or army of enforcement officials can deter every determined swindler.

Finally, it should be noted that the main problems of the Street today in a paradoxical fashion reflect the natural and healthy growth of the economy itself. The rise in new shareowners, the dramatic increase in business of the over-the-counter market which has yet to catch up with all the full disclosure rules of the exchanges, the influx of securities salesmen and brokers new to the industry, these and more make up the problems of the 1960's. Though these are matters of grave concern, they are a distant cry from the sordid corruption that infested Wall Street in the 1920's. Perhaps no better comparison can be made of the past and now than to note the tone of the latest investigation of the Street and the one that was held in 1933 and 1934. The latter investigation, conducted publicly by a U.S. Senate Committee, made daily headlines that shocked and appalled. The full-scale Securities and Exchange Commission investigation of 1961 and 1962, unlike its predecessor, is welcomed by most of the Street.* The headlines that it makes should not be anywhere as disturbing. To sum up, the Pecora hearings of 1933 and 1934 were a needed exposé. The S.E.C. investigation, though needed, is a relatively quiet study, supported generally by the Street itself.

It is at this point that we can at last answer the question posed almost thirty years ago by the man whose signature was the final deed that made the Securities and Exchange Act a law of the land. The moment of signing on June 6, 1934, was recalled by Ferdinand Pecora, counsel for the last great public investigation of Wall Street.

"There were six of us there. Senator Couzens, Senator Fletcher, Representative Rayburn, Tommy Corcoran, Ben Cohen and myself. The President used six pens to sign his name. When he had finished writing 'velt' he handed the last pen to me and said, 'Ferd, now that I have signed this bill and it has become law, what kind of law will it be?'

---

* The S.E.C. has been requested by Congress to complete its probe and make its final report by January, 1963. However, the commission has asked for an extension of time.

He smiled. I wasn't sure whether he wanted an answer. I realized finally that he did, and I replied, 'It will be a good or bad bill, Mr. President, depending upon the men who administer it.' "

One may add not only has this and other securities reform acts been ably enforced, but the Street itself has shown that the history of chicanery and stock manipulations that festered so easily and widely during the 1920's need not occur again.

INDEX